HELIOPOLIS
REBIRTH
OF THE
CITY OF THE SUN

AGNIESZKA DOBROWOLSKA

JAROSŁAW DOBROWOLSKI

THE AMERICAN UNIVERSITY IN CAIRO PRESS
CAIRO · NEW YORK

This publication has been produced with the financial assistance of the
European Union. The contents of this publication are the sole responsibility
of the authors and can under no circumstances be regarded as reflecting
the position of the European Union.

Copyright © 2006 by
The American University in Cairo Press
113 Sharia Kasr el Aini, Cairo, Egypt
420 Fifth Avenue, New York, NY 10018
www.aucpress.com

Dar el Kutub No. 23663/05
ISBN 977 416 008 8

Designed by Agnieszka Dobrowolska
Layout by Mervat Waheeb, Virgin Graphics
Printed in Egypt

CONTENTS

FOREWORD

The Cairo suburb of Heliopolis could be described as the most 'Mediterranean' part of the metropolis, although the most 'Levantine' is perhaps more accurate: Heliopolis is home to families who trace their origins back to Egypt, Greece, Lebanon, Armenia, Syria, Turkey, Sudan, and Italy, as well as many other countries.

Various nationalities and adherents to the three monotheistic faiths coexist in an ambiance of small shops that sell diamonds or rich imported perfumes alongside traditional workshops and markets. It is an environment that captivates the visitor immediately and contributes to a general atmosphere of tolerance and liveliness.

The suburb of Heliopolis was originally planned as a commercial enterprise by its initiator, the Belgian Baron Empain in 1905. He made his dream come true by establishing a modern city in the desert outside the crowded town of Cairo, much of which at the time still appeared medieval.

The history of Heliopolis as an inhabited place goes back many ages. The reader will be able to follow this historic account from its beginning in pharaonic times up to the present day, in which we now find the modern town that so gracefully reflects nineteenth-century trends in architecture and urban planning.

This book is the result of the project "Heliopolis: Where Egypt and Europe Meet," funded by the European Union. The Netherlands-Flemish Institute is grateful for this generous financial support, and by embracing this project, it hopes to contribute to the study and dissemination of important aspects of Egypt's modern history.

Dr. G. J. A. Borg,
Director of the Netherlands-Flemish Institute in Cairo

ACKNOWLEDGMENTS

The European Union's Delegation of the European Commission in Egypt ■
recognized Heliopolis as a place where Egypt and Europe have met for
the past hundred years in a variety of stimulating and fruitful ways. Without
its funding, this book would never have come into being. The work on
this project grew out of the activities of the Netherlands-Flemish Institute
in Cairo, and the enthusiastic support of its director Dr. Gert Borg was
essential to its success. The AUC Press then transformed the idea of the
book into reality—may all authors be blessed with a publisher like this.
During the fascinating adventure of writing this book we were fortunate
to benefit from the help and advice of many institutions and individuals.
We would like to give them all our heartfelt thanks, particularly:

The Heliopolis Company, who by allowing access to the precious
original material in the Company's archives gave us the chance to feel in
touch with the creators of Heliopolis.

Nagwa Shoeb of the Heliopolis Association for her encouragement
and many important insights.

Hoda Edward Mikhail of the Ministry of Housing for the professional
information she provided.

The Environmental and Remote Sensing Services Center, and especially
Ms. Mervat al-Jissri, for courteously allowing the use of a satellite image
of Heliopolis free of charge.

Dietrich ("Dyczek") Raue of the German Archaeological Institute for
patiently explaining the mysteries of ancient Egypt.

Samir Raafat for generously sharing his knowledge and permitting us
to use his photographic archives.

Robert Ilbert for his excellently researched *Heliopolis, genèse d'une ville*,
published in 1981, which was our principal source of information on the
Heliopolis Company's early history.

Patrick Godeau for providing the project with not only the photographic
skills that his assignment required, but a huge chunk of his heart and soul
as well.

Mervat Waheeb for contributing her talent and hard work to make the
book attractive.

Patrick Werr for making the text readable through his empathetic
editorial work.

We are profoundly grateful to our neighbors and the people of Heliopolis
for inspiration and for sharing their personal memories. And, although he
is no longer with us, we thank Baron Edouard Empain for building Heliopolis.
By doing so he not only added a rich contribution to Cairo, Mother of
the World, but also created a wonderful place for us to live in.

THE LOST CITY

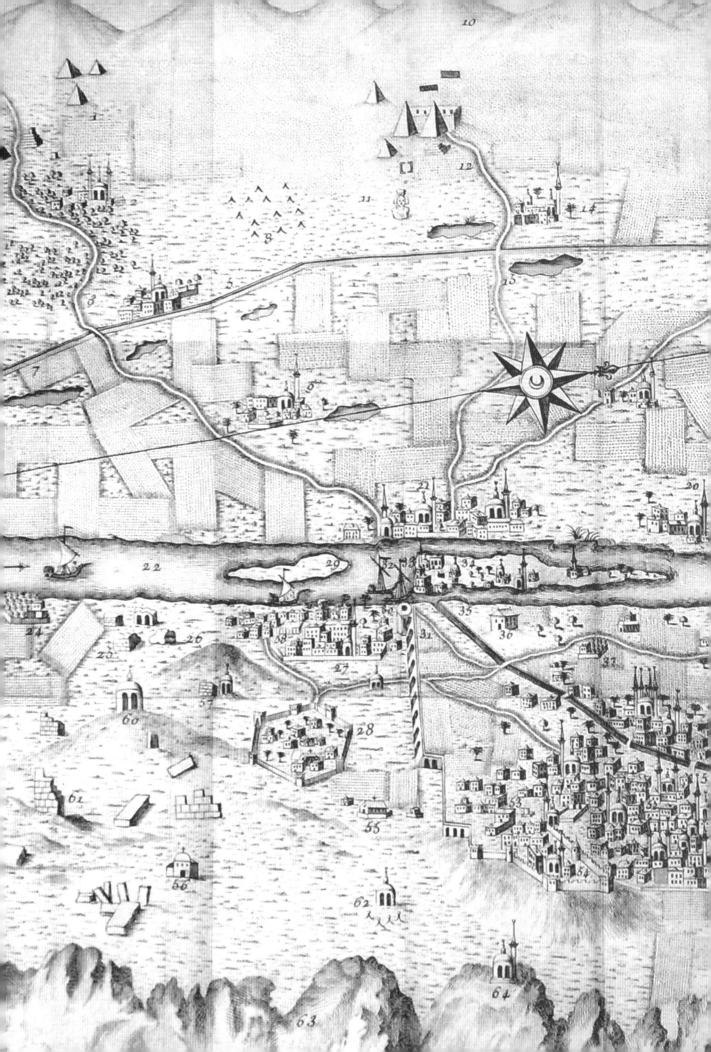

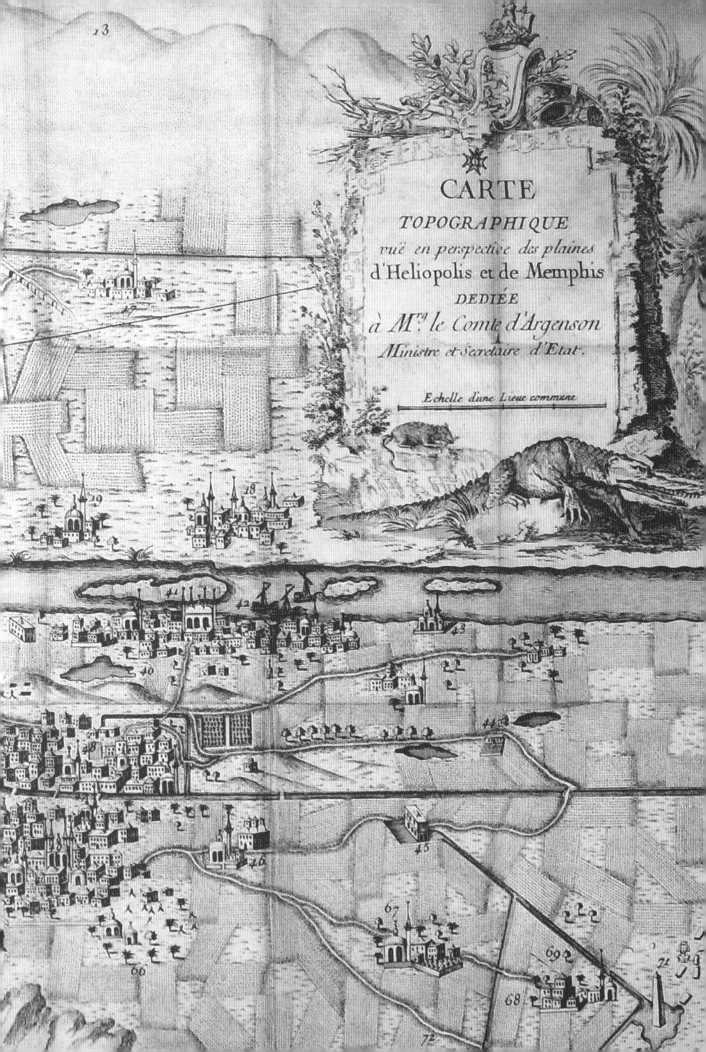

CARTE

TOPOGRAPHIQUE
vüe en perspective des plaines
d'Heliopolis et de Memphis
DEDIÉE
à M.^r le Comte d'Argenson
Ministre et Secretaire d'Etat.

Echelle d'une Lieue commune

Page 8 and 9: Satellite image of Heliopolis. North is on the right hand side.

Page 10: The obelisk of Heliopolis in an engraving by Georg Ebers from 1879.

Preceding pages: Map of Cairo and its environs from 1755 by Claude-Louis Fourmont. North is to the right. The pyramids of Giza and Saqqara are in the upper left corner, the obelisk of ancient Heliopolis in the lower right corner.

Above: Pascal Coste's watercolor of 1818 shows the obelisk of Heliopolis standing in a pond of water, surrounded by open landscape.

THE LOST CITY

The site of ancient Heliopolis lies in the Cairo suburb of Matariya, which straddles the metro line by the edge of modern Heliopolis. Matariya is a busy and densely populated middle and lower class district with streets packed with fast-moving minibuses, pick-up trucks, donkey-carts, and other vehicles of every description. Some fifteen or twenty meters beneath the maze of narrow, dusty streets lie buried the vast hidden remains of one of ancient Egypt's most important cities.

People had already lived here in predynastic times. Yet, apart from a few clues provided by a late-fourth-millennium B.C. cemetery, little is known about them. As soon as script was invented, however, Heliopolis entered the historical scene, for it was here that some of Egypt's most important religious texts were written. From this primeval time at the dawn of history come myths of the universal creation. Of the four separate cosmogonies that originated in Egypt's different religious centers, the one that developed in Heliopolis was the earliest, and it continued to influence theologians

throughout ancient Egyptian history. Here in Heliopolis, the central figure of the creation myth was the sun god and creator Atum, later identified with Ra, the divine Sun itself. From earliest times on, Heliopolis was the City of the Sun, and the solar cult originating here had a tremendous impact on ancient Egyptian religion.

It is perhaps appropriate that the majestic obelisk erected by the Middle Kingdom ruler Senwosert I (r. 1971–1926 B.C.) is the only significant surviving remnant of the ancient city and its grand temple, since this very form of monument appears to have originated in Heliopolis, which at some points had more obelisks than Thebes. An obelisk erected in a temple was the ultimate gift a king of Egypt, himself the 'Son of Ra,' could offer to his heavenly father and universal creator, the Sun. These giant monolithic blocks were carved of hard granite and shipped from the quarries of Aswan. At dawn, the obelisks' shining tips of precious metal would catch the first rays of the sun high above a land still engulfed by night. For many centuries they would continue to inspire awe and fascination, and because of this, the 1,000-kilometer journey down the Nile from Aswan to Heliopolis was just the beginning of further travels and adventures for many obelisks.

Such was the case with the famous twin 'Cleopatra's Needles.' These were originally erected by Thutmosis III some 3,500 years ago in the Heliopolis temple, which by that time was more than a thousand years old. In the year 12 B.C., Ceasar Augustus moved them to Alexandria, then Egypt's capital, to adorn the newly erected Ceasareum, the temple of the imperial cult. One of them was still standing upright when the Scottish traveler and artist David Roberts sketched them in September 1838. The other lay toppled nearby but remained in one piece. In 1877, the ruler of Egypt presented one of the two obelisks to the British government, which built a special barge to transport it to England. In a violent storm, however, the barge broke free from the ship towing it and was lost on the high seas.

Above: When the scholars and artists attached to Napoleon's army depicted and described "Cleopatra's Needles" around 1800, they could not have expected that thirty-three years later, an Egyptian obelisk would grace the Place de la Concorde in Paris.

"Cleopatra's Needles" in their
present locations:
above, in London;
opposite, in New York.

It seemed that Thutmosis' colossal offering to the sun god had been consigned forever to the dark depths of the sea. A few days later, however, it was found drifting in the Bay of Biscay and was transported safely to London. There, it was erected on the Victoria Embankment where it has since enjoyed as much sunshine as London can offer. Its twin traveled in 1879 to New York, where, more than a century after its uneventful journey, it continues to adorn Central Park.

Other obelisks grace Rome, Paris, and Istanbul. Of the world's twelve largest standing pharaonic obelisks, only four remain in Egypt. Some were carried off to Rome by the great Roman emperors. Later, in the year 390, Theodosius the Great, Christian emperor of the Roman East, took an obelisk of Thutmosis III to grace the hippodrome in Constantinople. Theodosius probably had no idea of its original symbolic significance or how the kings

Æliopolis. Cap. xv.

On dem König Busiris ist diese Statt Eliopolis / zu Teutsch Sonnenstatt / gebawen worden / vnd ist so groß gewesen daß jhr Ringkmawr vmb sich hat begriffen 140. Stadien / vnnd hat gehabt 100. Porten. Da haben vor alten zeiten die König Hof gehalten. Die Griechen haben diese Statt Thebas genennt / vnnd die Hebreer On / wie man in dem Propheten Ezechiel findt. Aber Ptolemeus der in Egyptē gewohnet hat etlich hundert jar vor Christi geburt / macht zwo Stett auß On vnd Eliopoli / wie das sein Cosmography anzeigt. Strabo schreibt von dieser Statt / daß sie auff einem Bühel ligt / vnd hat gehabt ein herrlichen Tempel / gebawen zu Ehren der Soñen. Es haben sich auch etwan in dieser Statt gehatten die Abgöttischen Priester / die Philosophi vnd Astronomi / vnd andere Gelehrte / die in grosser achtung vnd Freyheiten sind gewesen / von alten zeiten her / wie das angezeigt wird im Buch der Geschöpff. In dieser Statt war Dionysius zu zeiten da Christus am Creutz litte / vnnd da er sahe der Sonnen Finsternuß / erkennt er das Leyden Gottes / wie er selbst nachmals bekēnt hat / da er zum Christlichen Glauben bekehrt ward / vnd Bischoff zu Athen in Griechenlandt ward.

Babylon / Memphis / Alkair. Cap. xvj.

Sebastian Münster wrote in his book *Cosmographia,* published in Basel in 1574: "By king Busiris was built this city Eliopolis, in German called Sun City, and it was so huge that its encircling wall was considered to be 140 stadia long and have 100 gates. The king held his court there since the old times. The Greeks called the city Thebes and the Hebrews, On, as one finds in the Prophet Ezechiel. But Ptolemy, who lived in Egypt about a hundred years before Christ's birth, makes two cities of On and Eliopolis, as his *Cosmography* indicates. Strabo writes about this city that it lay on a hill and had a marvelous temple built to worship the sun. There were also in this city idolatrous priests who since the old times held philosophy and astronomy and other sciences there in great respect and freedom, as is related in the *Book of Creation.* Dionysius was in this city at the time when Christ was crucified, and there he saw the sun eclipsed and realized the God's suffering which he himself later professed when he converted to the Christian faith and was the bishop of Athens in Greece."

of Egypt erected obelisks to commemorate royal jubilees, victories, or other grand events. But apparently—just like Ceasar Augustus before him—he saw the obelisk as a symbol of authority and power, and, accordingly, had a pedestal built for it decorated with images that proclaimed his imperial glory.

With time, the memories of ancient Egypt faded further and further away, yet obelisks never ceased to captivate imaginations. Medieval Arab travelers had only fantastic ideas about their use: the tenth-century author al-Muqaddasi surmised that since crocodiles were a menace at the time of the obelisks' construction, their purpose was to offer magical protection against the beasts. Similarly, the popes who recycled the obelisks that had been brought to Rome in antiquity to adorn their apostolic capital knew as little about ancient Egyptian history as medieval Arab scholars. The same fascination with obelisks drove the French to carry a 250-ton block of granite all the way from Luxor to Paris, and then, 167 years later, in 2000, to cover its tip in gold, so that, once again, it can reflect the rays of the sun as it rises over the Place de la Concorde.

The obelisk that today commands the site of ancient Heliopolis is the oldest surviving in Egypt. The pink granite monument, towering 20.41 meters, is decorated with hieroglyphic texts containing King Senwosert's name and titles, and an exhortation: "May life be given to him for ever and ever." Senwosert's memory indeed lives on through his monuments, but the obelisk, once part of a great temple that thrived in the midst of a prosperous city, today stands in a vast, empty lot.

Heliopolis, called 'Iwnw' by the ancient Egyptians, was on par with the great Egyptian capital Memphis at a time when Thebes, later so mighty, was no more than a village. Outside the circle of Egyptologists, the city is known as 'On,' because that is how the Old Testament renders its name. The Bible relates how the pharaoh's permission for Joseph to marry Asenat, daughter of the high priest of On, marked his elevation to the highest position in Egypt after the king.

The reason for the city's ascendancy was apparently its strategic location. This was neatly summed up by ancient Greek visitors: "From the coast inland as far as Heliopolis the breadth of Egypt is considerable, the country is flat . . . and full of swamps" (Herodotus, 5th century B.C.); "After Heliopolis is the 'Nile above Delta.' The country on the right hand, as you go up the Nile, is called Libya. . . . the country on the left hand is called Arabia." (Strabo, 24 B.C.).

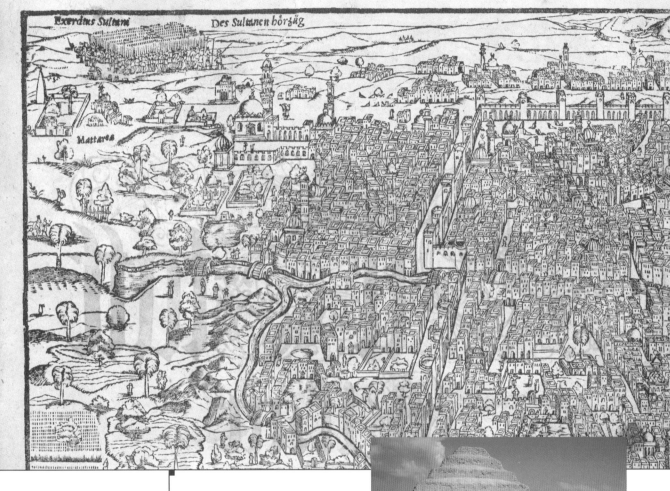

Above: Sebastian Münster's map, based on one by Matteo Pagano from 1549, shows the highly imaginary view of the pyramids in Giza (right), the obelisk of Heliopolis in Matariya (upper left), as well as the medieval walls of Cairo, where many of the stones from Heliopolis temples ended. *Inset:* The Step Pyramid of Saqqara.

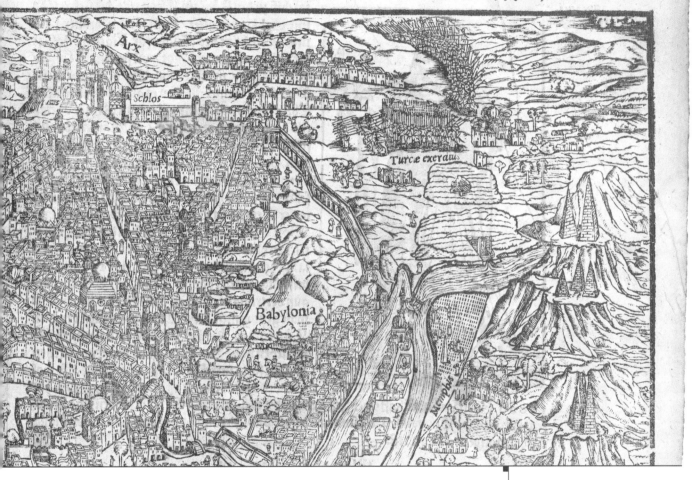

btigen bnd besten Statt Alkair. Occccxxxbij

A little more evidence exists from a second grand phase of
development—between 2350 and 2300 B.C. under the Sixth Dynasty—
but not on the original site. Following a custom as old as the Old Kingdom
itself, of quarrying old monuments for building material, the medieval rulers
of Islamic Egypt used stone blocks from Heliopolis in their construction
projects in Cairo. They can be seen, with their hieroglyphic inscriptions
still visible, in the mosque of al-Hakim finished in A.D. 1013, or in the
defense walls of Cairo built in 1087–92 by Badr al-Din al-Gamali, vizier
of the Caliph al-Mustansir.

The first known temple of the early city was built by King Djoser (r.
2630–2611 B.C.). In the long run, the temple didn't fare as well as Djoser's
other project, the sixty-meter-high Step Pyramid at Saqqara, which was
the first pyramid ever built. The Saqqara monument still overlooks the
Nile Valley, but of his Heliopolis temple only a few stone objects remain.

■23

The early temples in Heliopolis were enlarged and added to for centuries, and together they eventually formed one of the biggest religious complexes in Egypt, rivaling those of Luxor or Memphis in size and splendor. The Middle Kingdom temple in which Senwosert erected his obelisk represented only one phase of this development. The temple's great enclosure of mud-brick walls once covered more then five square kilometers. As recently as 1799, Messrs Lancret and Du Bois-Aym of the Napoleonic expedition could write: "The enclosure of the city is still very much recognizable; built of mud brick, it is enormous. In some places it stands up to eighteen meters."

Although the edifices have now all but disappeared, we can still piece together an idea of how they looked by augmenting the scarce material excavated by archaeologists with descriptions by ancient visitors.

"There, too, is Heliopolis situated upon a large mound. It contains the temple of the Sun and the ox, Mneyis, which is kept in sanctuary . . . At the entrance into the temenos is a paved floor, in breadth about a plethrum, or even less; its length is three or four times as great, and in some instances even more. . . . throughout the whole length on each side are placed stone sphinxes, at the distance of twenty cubits or a little more from each other . . . next after the sphinxes is a large propylon, then on proceeding further, another propylon, and then another . . . " wrote the Greek geographer Strabo in 24 B.C.

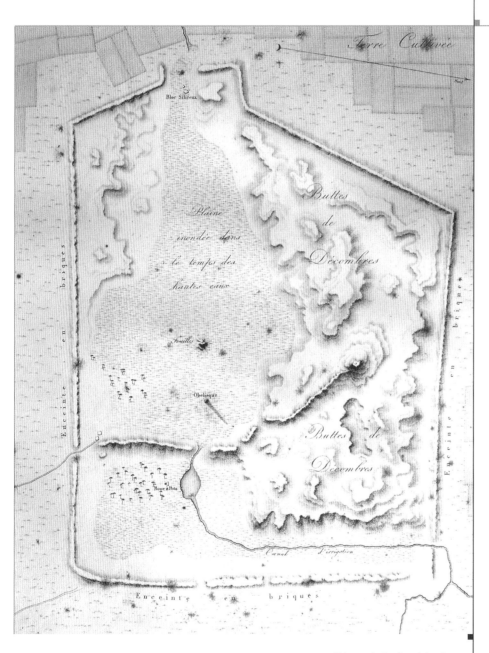

This map in the *Description de l'Egypte*, surveyed about 1800, shows just mounds of earth and the lonely obelisk inside the ancient enclosure of Heliopolis. The site was still impressive.

The temple must have been impressive. One can imagine the length of its white façade stretching for more than a kilometer, with at least three portals flanked with scarlet door jambs and lintels, surrounded by dozens of obelisks. Its colored stones, striking in their contrast, were taken from nearby quarries—whitewashed walls of limestone from the Muqattam hills; sandstone pillars, thresholds, and lintels, ranging golden beige to deep red, from Gebel al-Ahmar; other pieces crafted from black basalt from Abu Zaa'bal. Yet for the classical-minded Strabo, "there was nothing pleasing or easily described, but rather a display of labor wasted."

The temple was more than a complex of impressive buildings: it was a huge economic enterprise as well. The elaborate rituals performed there required not only an army of priests of different ranks, but also numerous administrative and productive personnel. Farmers, fishermen, and herdsmen worked vast land holdings that provided the many kinds of animals, plants, food, and drink required for offerings. An array of scribes kept track of the economic activities. Bakers, butchers, and brewers as well as weavers

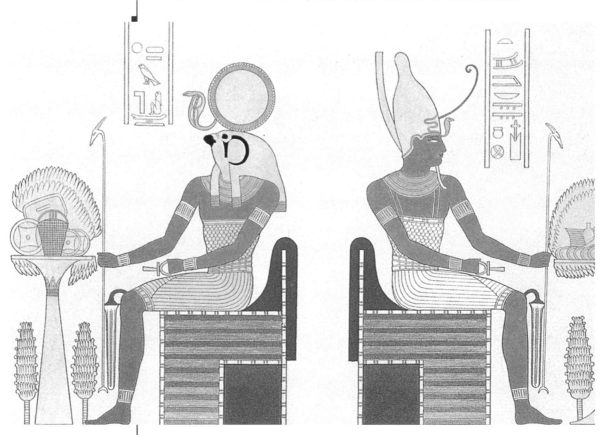

Colorful renderings in the *Description de l'Egypte* of religious scenes depicted on the walls of the tomb of Ramesses III in the Valley of the Kings .

and sandal makers fed and clothed the temple personnel. They were kept busy: an account from the time of Ramesses III recorded 12,963 people in the permanent employ of the Temple of Ra in Heliopolis, a number that did not include the numerous women who also worked there. Nor did it include the construction crews who constantly repaired, remodeled, or enlarged the temple. Among these were stonecutters, masons, and carpenters who built walls; carvers, sculptors, and painters who decorated them; and workers and animals who moved stone, brick, and earth, provided water, and brought supplies for the huge teams. The temple world was a microcosm within Egyptian society, and running an enterprise like the Heliopolis temple was big business.

Much of this activity had long vanished by the time Strabo visited. "At present, the city is entirely deserted," he wrote. But Strabo, a Greek intellectual, had special reason to visit Heliopolis: he was following in the footsteps of his great mentors (or at least he believed so).

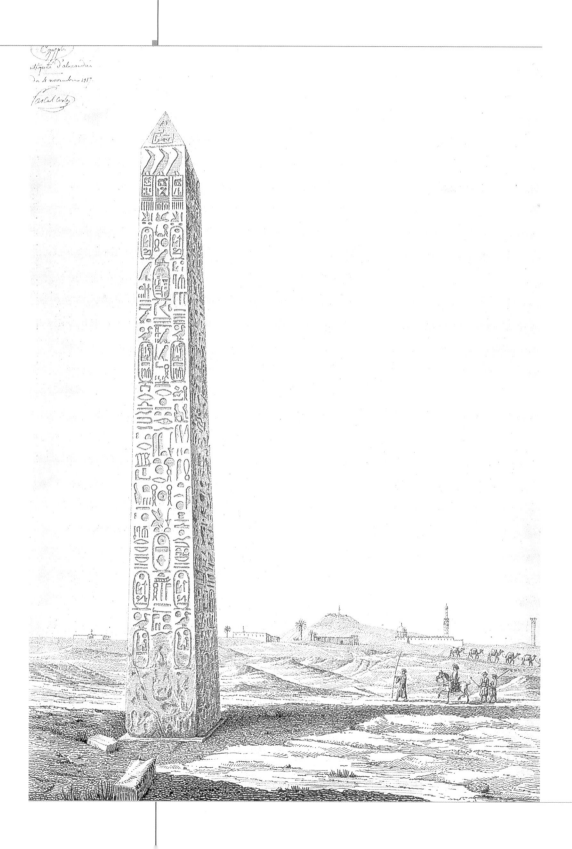

"At Heliopolis we saw . . . the residences of Plato and of Eudoxus . . . Eudoxus came here with Plato, and, according to some writers, lived thirteen years in the society of the priests. For the latter were distinguished for their knowledge of heavenly bodies, but were mysterious and uncommunicative . . . "

Plato himself did not leave any record of a sojourn in Egypt. Nevertheless, Strabo's attitude was typical: Egypt was believed to be the source of profound knowledge, a source from which Greek philosophers could draw, and Heliopolis was considered a repository of this knowledge.

By Strabo's time, Egypt had long been under Greek or Roman rule, and the ancient Egyptian gods were now worshiped in a Hellenized guise. The concept of a god-like king conveniently merged with the idea of the Roman emperor representing divine power. Egyptian gods were assimilated into the Greek pantheon, and these included a deity worshiped specifically at Heliopolis, a heron named Benu buried in the ashes that for the Greeks became the phoenix reborn from his funeral pyre in the Arabian desert every six hundred years. Ra himself was identified with the Greek sun god Helios, and so the city was given its classical name, Heliopolis.

In 383, the Christian emperor Theodosius, seeking to stamp out the last vestiges of paganism, ordered the closure of all pagan temples throughout the Empire. The Egyptians at the time were absorbed in theological disputes about the nature of Christ and had little time for the ancient gods, now perceived as pagan demons. The glory and prosperity of ancient On had come to an end.

Yet the ruins, especially Senowsert's great obelisk, continued to inspire wonder in visitors. Arab travelers were fascinated by obelisks, even though they couldn't agree on what to call them. Early geographers spoke of "columns" *(ustuwanat)*, later authors, including the famous al-Maqrizi, of "pillars" *(awamid)*, travelers from Iran and Andalusia, of "minarets" *(manarat)*. The present word in Arabic is *misalla*, literally, a large needle. Several authors who visited Heliopolis in the mid-eleventh century mentioned that moisture from condensation seeped continuously in all seasons from beneath the copper top of the obelisk, causing moss and other vegetation to grow miraculously high above the ground on the barren granite of the obelisk. In about 1195, at the time of the visit by the scholar and scientist 'Abd al-Latif al-Baghdadi, Heliopolis was still recognizable as an ancient town, and many statues were still standing, one of which was fifteen meters high.

29

One of the two mighty obelisks had already collapsed: "It was broken
in two pieces by the fall, owing to its excessive weight. The copper which
had covered the top had been taken away," al-Baghdadi wrote.

The ruins attracted the attention of various travelers, who described,
drew, painted, and studied them. Nevertheless, over the centuries the
remnants of ancient Heliopolis slowly vanished. "In a space of a kilometer
square, surrounded by walls of crude brick, which now appear like ridges
of earth, were situated the sacred edifices of Heliopolis. . . . statues

and the broken obelisk, probably, now lie beneath accumulated soil.—Such are the poor remains of Heliopolis, " wrote E. W. Lane in November 1825. At the time it was quite a journey from Cairo: "The route from Musr to the site of Heliopolis lies along the desert; but near the limits of the cultivable soil. . . . On the left of the route is a large settlement of courtesans, composing a complete village. Passengers generally attract several of these girls from their huts; and are often much annoyed by their importunity." Today, there is just a residential district there, with people living their everyday lives. The many little girls, who will follow any foreigner, are just asking for small gifts: "Pen, pen, mister. Give me a pen."

Wrote Lane, "This part of the desert is a sandy flat, strewed with pebbles, and with petrified wood." That was quite a difference from the times when Herodotus, visiting in the fifth century B.C., complained about mosquitoes in Heliopolis, then surrounded by lush vegetation. In the mid-nineteenth century the landscape changed again when the governor of Egypt, Muhammad 'Ali, reclaimed the area for agricultural land. Later in the nineteenth and early twentieth centuries, Matariya became an upscale suburb for the new bourgeoisie, spearheaded by British residents who built houses and villas in the area. The mosquitoes were back.

Then the ever-expanding metropolis engulfed it all. Only Senwosert's lonely obelisk in the middle of a vast empty lot endures as a reminder of the lost city of On. Heliopolis, the birthplace of the phoenix ever rising from the ashes, was to be resurrected elsewhere.

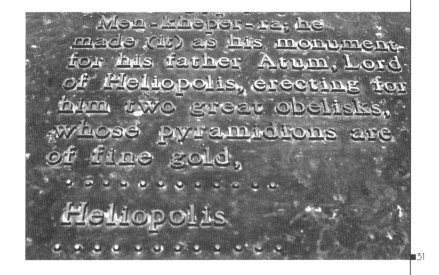

Men - kheper - ra; he made (it) as his monument for his father Atum, Lord of Heliopolis, erecting for him two great obelisks, whose pyramidions are of fine gold,

. . . .

Heliopolis

. . . .

THE CITY
REBORN

Paris 25 Févr 1908

L'ARCHITECTE SOUSSIGNÉ

PALA

DE S.A. LE PRINCE HVSSEIN

— FACADE EST —

ECHELLE DE 0.01=1.00

SOCIÉTÉ FRANÇAISE
D'ENTREPRISES EN EGYPTE
——
Direction technique:
13, Rue Soliman Pacha
30/3/08

Above: A tower in a residential
building on Ibrahim al-Laqqani
Street, drawn in 2000.

Preceding pages: 1908 design drawing by architect Alexandre Marcel of the façade of Prince Hussein's palace, now in the archives of the Heliopolis Company.

THE CITY REBORN

An old adage says that when a man has fathered a child, planted a tree, and built a house he has truly left behind a mark for posterity. Many people can achieve that, but how many, other than mighty rulers, have built not just a house, but created a city? The industrialist Baron Edouard Empain provides such an example, for Heliopolis exists due to his vision and single-handed perseverance.

Empain once invited the Belgian architect Ernest Jaspar, then a young man, for a riding trip to the desert off the Suez road. According to a story related by Jaspar's son, the industrialist pointed toward a vast empty plateau and said:

I want to build a city here. It will be called Heliopolis, a city of the sun . . . I want it to be magnificent. I wish that the architecture will conform to the tradition of this country. I am looking for a specialist of Islamic art. You like the mosques, you are an architect; would you submit a concept design?

Above: Baron Edouard Empain,
1852–1929.

Opposite: Entrance to a Paris
subway station.

Any architect would have his breath taken away at such a prospect. Jaspar's heart must have missed a beat. The vision was broad and the enterprise daring, yet it was not folly or fantasy—it belonged to a businessman with his feet firmly on the ground.

The son of a Belgian village schoolteacher, Baron Empain was emblematic of the nineteenth-century giants who pushed the innovations of the Industrial Revolution to their limits—one of the builders of the financial and technical bases for the age of steam and electricity. He was eventually to become a close friend of the Belgian king, accumulate an immense fortune, and even be made an army general during the First World War. He established a business empire that remains until today one of the biggest financial groups worldwide. Indeed, by constructing railroads and pioneering electricity-powered transport systems, he was at the very core of what the industrial nations proudly hailed as their triumphal "march of progress."

Edouard Empain, born in 1852 in Beloeil, Belgium to a large family, had to work his way through school. He graduated as an engineer from the Metallurgic Society in Brussels and at age twenty-five got a job as a draftsman, then later as a quarry operator. He soon put his extraordinary business talents to work, however, and his business interests expanded rapidly. Seeing Belgium's underdeveloped transport system as a business opportunity, he built the country's first local railway and established the Compagnie generale des tramways à voie étroite. To help finance his projects, he set up the Banque Empain, renamed the Banque Industrielle Belge in 1881, which became the financial base of his business empire. He soon became involved in the railway business in France, an involvement that culminated in his participation in the construction of the Paris subway (Metro) in the 1890s. Even as late as 1937, *Time* magazine wrote that Empain's son was the "principal owner of the Paris Metro." In the early 1900s, Empain created companies to generate and distribute electricity in various French and Belgian cities, and by 1904 he was busy building railroads in Congo. By grafting his transport and electricity businesses together, he built and operated electricity-powered urban transport systems in Naples, Turin, Madrid, Warsaw, China, and Egypt.

10 MAY 2001
BÂTIMENTS DE PARIS

Baron Haussmann's modernization infused new life into Paris when it brought open spaces, greenery, and modern infrastructure into the city of picturesque old buildings.

In Egypt in 1894, Empain established a subsidiary, the Société Anonyme Tramways du Caire, with Belgian partner Jules Urban, and six months later their first Egyptian tramway line was up and running. At the time, relations between the Belgian embassy and the Khedival court were good, and many Belgian businessmen were active in Egypt. The Empain Group also ran two other Egyptian companies: the Société Anonyme de chemins de fer à voie étroite de Basse Egypte and the Menzaleh Canal and Navigation Company Ltd. As usual, Empain enlisted well-connected people from broad backgrounds, including influential people from the Belgian colonies, resident British clerks to liaise with local authorities, and French experts who had helped construct the Paris Metro. He took on projects that responded to local needs and he cultivated good relations with the Khedival court and the local government. Building on his success in transport, with the Heliopolis project Empain turned for the first time to real estate development.

The Cairo of 1900 was vastly different from the cities and temples of ancient Egypt—or even the Islamic city that E. W. Lane and other early-nineteenth-century travelers described. The Egyptian ruler Khedive Ismail, when young, had been sent to Paris to study when the French capital was still essentially medieval, a maze of dirty winding streets in close and crowded districts, a city where the walls of the opera house had not yet begun to rise. From 1853 onward, Baron Haussmann's sweeping urban improvements had cut wide boulevards through the city blocks, and by 1870 some 150 kilometers of brand new streets had been extended, more than 16 square kilometers of parks laid out, and a modern water supply system and more than 600 kilometers of sewers installed. On consecutive visits to the city, Ismail had watched as the new Paris emerged.

Ismail was determined to rejuvenate his own capital in a similar way, and in the 1860s began to turn Cairo into his own 'Paris on the Nile.' To a large degree he succeeded. The Cairo opera house, though not a match for the grand Parisian edifice of Jean-Louis-Charles Garnier, nevertheless opened six years later. Although some straight, wide alleys were cut through Cairo's earlier districts, unlike Napoleon III, Khedive Ismail did not need to order large-scale demolitions to create his modern city. The new downtown was built on sparsely built-up land containing mostly gardens that had emerged when the course of the Nile gradually shifted west, away from the old city. By 1900, Cairo was a thriving modern town, and the surrounding land was being rapidly developed: the leafy district of Garden City was laid out, the Swiss had begun upgrading the district of Zamalek on a Nile island, and Helwan was linked with the city by a railway and developed into a stylish spa district. Land prices soared as people rushed to buy and speculate on lots along the Nile.

With real estate prices reaching the levels of Brussels or Paris, the transport magnate Empain had a clever idea: buy cheap, outlying land, then provide a convenient way to get to and from downtown. The name of the company created to carry it out reflected the idea: The Cairo Electric Railways and Heliopolis Oases Company. Empain had been sponsoring the excavations of a Belgian archaeologist Jean Capart, which possibly influenced the idea that the new project should revive the ancient city of Heliopolis, but his main incentive was no doubt hard business calculations.

According to an account of one of the Khedive's descendants, the Belgian businessman applied for an audience with the Khedive Abbas Hilmi II, who was ruler of Egypt at the time. When members of Abbas Hilmi's family later inquired what the foreigner had wanted, the khedive replied that he merely asked for a piece of the desert. The princesses were surprised to learn the Belgian was actually prepared to pay for it, too!

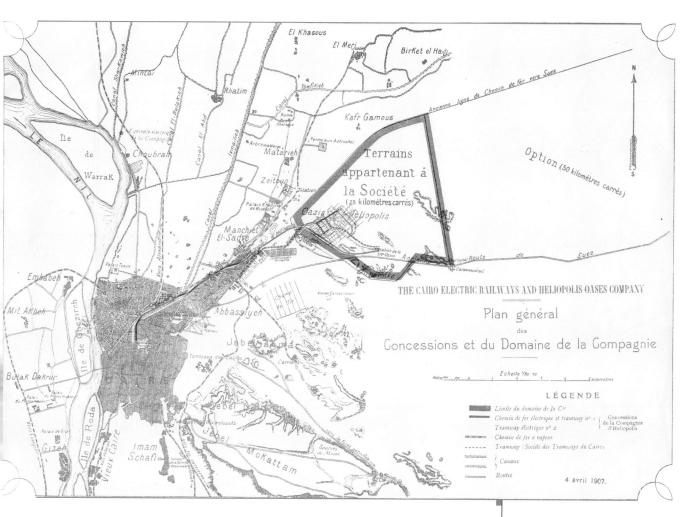

Documents from the Heliopolis
Company's archives.

Above: A 4 April 1907 plan of the
land purchased by the Company.

Following page: Pages from a 1908
copy of Khedive Abbas Hilmi II's
decree creating the Cairo
Electric Railways and Heliopolis
Oases Company, and from a
30 September 1908 copy of the
preliminary contract between
Boghos Nubar Pasha and
Édouard Empain.

R.P. 634

Extrait

au Supplément du "Journal
Officiel" du 24 Février 1906 N° 20 annexé
à l'Acte authentique de dépôt de documents reçu en ce Greffe le 7 Mars
1906 sub N° 8750 rectifié par acte
reçu en ce même Greffe le 24 Septembre 1908 sub N° 12808, par "The
Cairo Electric Railways
& Heliopolis Oases Company".

———

Supplément au "Journal Officiel"
N° 20 du Samedi 24 Février 1906.

Partie Officielle

The Cairo Electric Railways
& Heliopolis Oases Company
(Société Anonyme)

Décret.

Nous, Khédive d'Egypte,
Vu l'acte préliminaire d'association sous seing privé le 23 Janvier 1906

---

le 23 Mai 1905 par le
Gouvernement Egyptien.
Omissis.

Statuts.

Titre premier.
Omissis.

Titre II.
Apports, fonds social, actions, obligations.
Art. 6.
Son Excellence Boghos Nubar
Pacha et Mr. Edouard Empain
font gratuitement apport à la présente
Société qui accepte :
1° De la concession de la construction
et de l'exploitation d'un chemin
de fer à traction électrique pour le
transport des voyageurs destiné à
relier au Pont Limoun (au Caire)
les terrains dits : "Oasis du désert
de l'Abbassieh" telle qu'ils l'ont
obtenu du Gouvernement Egyptien
par l'acte de concession en date

---

au Caire, entre les Sieurs :
Omissis.

Acte préliminaire d'association.

Entre :
1° S.E. Boghos Pacha Nubar,
propriétaire, demeurant au Caire ;
2° Mr. Edouard Empain, ingénieur,
demeurant 33, rue du Congrès, à Bruxelles ;
3° @ 222. Omissis.
Il a été convenu :
de former, sauf approbation du Gouvernement, une Société Anonyme dénommée
The Cairo Electric Railways and
Heliopolis Oases Company, régie
par les Statuts ci-annexés et ayant
pour objet principal la mise en valeur
et l'exploitation des concessions accordées
par le Gouvernement Egyptien le 23 Mai
1905 pour un chemin de fer électrique
et deux lignes de tramways électriques,
ainsi que des terrains comprenant
2500 (deux mille cinq cents) hectares
dans le désert de l'Abbassieh vendus

Omissis.
"Pour copie conforme à
l'original délivrée à la requête
de Mr. Carton de Wiart pour
servir à The Cairo Electric Railways & Heliopolis Oases Company
(Société Anonyme).
Caire le 30 Septembre 1908
Le Greffier

Although the company paid a mere one Egyptian pound per feddan, it nevertheless spent a total five thousand pounds for the land alone, a substantial sum at the time. The legal agreement was signed by His Excellency Boghos Nubar Pasha, a property owner residing in Cairo, and Mr. Edouard Empain, engineer, residing at 33, du Congrès St., Bruxelles, according to a preliminary document preserved in the Heliopolis Company archives. It was agreed to create, the document states:

> "pending the government's approval, the Société Anonyme named The Cairo Electric Railways and Heliopolis Oases Company, governed by its own status, with the principal objective being to establish and exploit the concession approved by the Egyptian Government on 23 May, 1905 for a railroad and two electric tramway lines.

The Société would make use of:
> The laws, benefits, and advantages of the contract dated 23 May, 1905, through which the Government of Egypt sold, yielded, and transferred rights to all the property of the area of 25 square kilometers, the equivalent of 2500 hectares or 5652 feddans, in the desert of Abbasiya, southeast from the ancient road to Suez."

The Heliopolis Oases Company was officially established eight months later on 23 January, 1906 with a capital of 15 million Belgian Francs. The decree was signed by Khedive Abbas Hilmi II and Prime Minister Mustafa Fahmy. The company also had to obtain the permission of the British, who had taken administrative control of Egypt in 1882 without ever declaring it a formal colony. In 1906, the iron-fisted Lord Cromer was consul general, and he kept a tight rein on the country that straddled the Suez Canal, a strategic choke point along Britain's shipping lanes to India. Only eight years earlier, Lord Kitchener, himself a future consul general in Cairo, had crushed the Mahdist rebellion in Sudan and, in Egypt, Cromer was worried by mounting nationalist feelings. In the end, the British proved not to be an obstacle, and the British adviser to the Ministry of Public Works, Sir William Garstin, signed off on Empain's project. It was then that the phoenix began rising once again from the ashes.

Above: Aerial view of central
Heliopolis, late 1920s.

Opposite: The tower of a
residential building on Baghdad
Street (former Boulevard Isma'il).

The site, ten kilometers from Cairo and close to the road to Suez in the desert of Abbasiya, had been carefully chosen. On a plateau above the Nile Valley, it was swept by cool, refreshing breezes from the north, yet protected by the Muqattam hills from the hot winds that occasionally blew from the south, making it warmer in winter and cooler in summer than elsewhere around Cairo. Even today, it is not unusual to leave the blue skies and crisp air of Heliopolis on a winter morning only to encounter humid and misty weather as you move closer to the Nile downtown.

Among the first buildings to be constructed was the company headquarters, located on the newly laid out Boulevard Abbas. In 1908 the company employed sixty-five people, twenty of them hired directly from Brussels and Paris, and covering all the major positions—director, deputy directors, engineering staff, and secretaries. All employees received

Opposite: The Heliopolis Company's headquarters on Ibrahim al-Laqqani Street, formerly Boulevard Abbas.

In the margin: "C.E.R." stands for Cairo Electric Railways on a mosaic in the pavement in front of the Company headquarters' main door.

free lodging in Heliopolis, although the director's palace was far plusher than the flats occupied by office clerks and workmen. Employees were also given free passage to work on the tramway, although engineers hired locally were confined to second class. Attitudes were colonial—early records mention no Muslim or female names among the employees, and the locally hired staff were mostly guards, drivers, and office boys. Even though Empain, to whom the Belgian King awarded the title of baron a year after the Heliopolis Company was formed, had declared, "I wish that the architecture will conform to the tradition of this country," he chose for his own palace an Indian style completely unrelated to any local tradition.

Much has changed in Heliopolis, Egypt, and Cairo in the hundred years since the Heliopolis Company was established, yet its headquarters, which still occupy the same building on Boulevard Abbas, now Ibrahim al-Laqqani Street, remain little affected. Tenants continue to pay their rent in the same spacious office hall, its impressive interior much as it always has been. Upstairs in the busy administration and development offices lie splendid pieces of furniture unaltered from the company's early days. Magnificent padded doors lead to the offices of senior officials, and fireplaces and original woodwork in the tall windows mix with the equipment typical of an Egyptian government office: metal desks, computers, and utensils for tea and coffee. On the walls, calendars show the holy Kaaba in Mecca or the Virgin Mary, depending on the clerk's religious faith. More than 1,200 people now work in the company's technical, administrative, financial, and real estate departments, including many women.

Opposite: The tower of a residential building at No 10, Ibrahim al-Laqqani Street (formerly Boulevard Abbas).

Some fifty years after army colonels led by Gamal Abd al-Nasser seized power in Egypt and later nationalized the Company, the country has become a very different place from the Egypt of Khedive Abbas and of Lord Cromer. Still, Egyptians generally do not look on Baron Empain as the quintessential colonialist. They prefer to see him as a man whose life became so inextricably bound up with their country that he chose to be buried in the basilica that he built in Heliopolis, and who left behind a magnificent contribution to Cairo's long, illustrious history. Asked about old Heliopolis, the Company's chief architect exclaims enthusiastically, "I love Baron Empain, because of two things: he built Heliopolis and he loved Egypt."

The view from Baron Empain's palace looking northwest onto Nazih Khalifa Street (formerly Avenue Baron Empain), in the 1920s and in 2006. The palace of Prince Hussein (later, Sultana Malak) is to the right, the Basilica in the background.

The northeastern corner of the Basilica (formerly Queen Elisabeth) Square, in the 1920s and 2006. This used to be the dividing line between the luxurious section of Heliopolis (to the left), and more modest housing (to the right).

Boulevard Abbas (now Ibrahim
al-Laqqani Street). The picture
from around 1930 shows the
Luna Park amusement center
where Roxy Square is today. The
picture from 2006 shows the
building on the corner of
Damascus Street (former
Boulevard Tawfiq) after alterations
during the 1930s.

View on Boulevard Abbas (now
Ibrahim al-Laqqani Street) from
the crossing at Avenue des
Pyramides in the 1920s and 2006.
To the left, the Heliopolis House
Hotel, with Groppi's terrace.

Views from the 1930s and 2006
of Boulevard Isma'il, now Baghdad
Street. The arcades still house
some of Heliopolis's most elegant
shops.

Al-Kurba Square in the 1920s
and in 2006; perhaps the least
altered urban space in Heliopolis.

The Avenue of the Pyramids
looking towards the Basilica, in
the 1930s and in 2006. Some of
the architecture survives, but of
the greenery, little remains.

Baron Empain's palace in the
1930s and in 2006.

THE
BUILDINGS
SPEAK

PARIS LE 1909

HÉLIOPOLIS OA
IMMEVBLE SVR LE
FACADE SVR L'AVENV
ECHELLE DE 0ᵐ02 = 1ᵐ00

S
57.
L'HYPPODROME.

Preceding pages: Design drawing for building No 2, Boulevard Abbas, the façade facing Roxy Square.

Above: Colonnaded arcades on Ibrahim al-Laqqani Street, formerly Boulevard Abbas.

THE BUILDINGS SPEAK

The rays of the sun slide daily over the façades and across the domes of Heliopolitan buildings, revealing and accentuating various architectural elements in an ever-changing play of shadow and light. The grand show is a testament to how appropriately Edouard Empain named the city he created, Heliopolis—the City of the Sun. He wanted it to be *magnifique*, and he succeeded.

In 1849, John Ruskin, the profoundly influential British author, artist, and critic, whose views on art continue to inspire even today, wrote, "Architecture is the art which so disposes and adorns the edifices raised by man . . . that the sight of them contributes to his mental health, power and pleasure." By this definition, there are many buildings around the world that fall into the category of non-architecture. Unfortunately, this includes vast areas of modern Cairo, where structural concrete frames have been filled with bare red bricks and where economy, not beauty, has been the driving force. So unlike the Heliopolis of a century ago. Whether or not one appreciates the orientalist forms of its buildings, accepts the clothing of European design concepts in eastern costumes, or admires the blending of modernity with historicism, one thing remains certain: the original Heliopolis was, and still is, a very powerful architectural statement. To understand its significance, one needs to look at what was happening in European architecture at the time Heliopolis was conceived.

Above: Galleria Vittorio Emmanuele in Milan, finished in 1877.

Right: Frontispiece of the 1738 English translation of Andrea Palladio's treatise on architecture.

YEAR 1900:
A CENTURY ENDS

In classical architecture, the categories by which buildings ought to be judged, according to Andrea Palladio, a theoretician and master neo-classical architect, were established by the first-century B.C. Roman architect and theoretician Pollio Marcus Vitruvius. "Three things according to Vitruvius ought to be considered," wrote Palladio in 1570, "and these are the utility or convenience, duration, and beauty." Since the Renaissance's rediscovery of classical architecture, these categories had been the criteria by which buildings were judged.

The nineteenth century wrought unprecedented changes in the ways architecture was used. Railway and subway stations, grand exhibition halls, department stores, and other new types of buildings required new architectural forms to reflect the new "utility." People likewise expected their homes to be connected to modern sewer systems, water supply mains, and electricity grids, while new means of transportation and communication allowed them more freedom as to where to live. Structures made of steel and reinforced concrete provided radically new means with which to achieve "duration." And finally (not without John Ruskin's influence), the meaning of "beauty" began to change. First the Gothic Revival and then a whole array of historic styles freed architecture from the classical canon. In place of the earlier notion that art should conform to established norms, aesthetic ideas appeared that demanded it celebrate individual creativity and reflect abstract, universal values as perceived from Nature.

The architecture of Barcelona's
Eixample district embodies the
spirit of the Belle Époque.

The First World War would soon shatter the European order and change societies forever, ushering in the revolutionary modernism that would strip architecture of all ornament and flood the world with identical box-like buildings. But 1900 was still a different era.

Architects from the École des Beaux-Arts in Paris, the most famous architectural school of the nineteenth century, were leaders of the movement that blended modern utility with handsome, classical forms. They used a traditional vocabulary of architectural elements—columns and domes, classical moldings, and formal and symmetrical façades—and their buildings were laid out on strictly regular plans, with great care taken to ensure "convenience or utility" as Vitruvius would have it. At the same time, they experimented with new materials, employing iron, steel, and glass in combination with masonry in such buildings as les Halles, the central market of Paris, constructed in 1854–66. Some of the finest examples of the style are the Grand Palais and the Petit Palais, both in Paris and built by architect Charles-Louis Girault in about 1900. The new Paris that emerged after Haussmann laid out the grand boulevards (designed by Victor Baltard, the architect of les Halles) was essentially a Beaux Arts city. Germany, Austria, England, and Italy followed, and edifices such as the Galleria Vittorio Emanuele in Milan, the Houses of Parliament in Berlin, and the Burgtheater in Vienna appeared throughout Europe. The buildings were costumed in historical styles such as neoclassical, neo-renaissance, or neo-baroque (which would be prevalent around the year 1900), but also in other styles, especially Gothic, as in the houses of parliament in London and Budapest.

This page: In a turn-of-the-century building in Milan, classical motifs mask a steel structure behind. In structures like the Eiffel Tower in Paris, such adornments were abandoned altogether.

Opposite: The Secession Pavilion in Vienna.

Occasionally, structures erected with new technologies to house new functions abandoned the historical costume altogether. Among these were structures built for the great industrial exhibitions of the time. As early as 1851, the famous Crystal Palace at the Great Exhibition in London was built entirely of iron and glass. Perhaps the most spectacular example is engineer Gustav Eiffel's 300-meter tower erected for the 1889 exhibition in Paris. The Palais des Machines at the same exhibition, by Ferdinand Dutert, was constructed from prefabricated trussed arches and enclosed a remarkable space of 117 by 46 meters in a single hall without internal supports. Such structures were nevertheless often dressed in a Beaux-Arts costume, as can be seen for instance in the Quai d'Orsay railway station that has now been converted into a museum to display arts from the period.

By the end of the nineteenth century, many young artists and architects saw mainstream academic tradition as a corset from which architecture should be liberated. The ferment reverberated throughout Europe, and the names—Secession, Stile Liberty, Art Nouveau, Jugendstil—reflected the counter-establishment character of the new style of free expression as it spread to different countries. The façade of the Secession Pavilion in Vienna, a building emblematic of the style, proclaims in bronze letters, "To each age, its art. To art, its freedom." (There will always be people who think that freedom is dangerous: the Nazis removed the inscription in 1938; it was only reinstalled after the war.)

Above: Art Nouveau permeates
the Eixample district in Barcelona,
from monumental buildings to
lamp-posts.

Opposite: A student of
architecture at the Glasgow
School of Art, 2005.

The style drew from the experience of the Arts and Crafts movement, which emphasized informality, modesty, structural integrity, and faithfulness to the natural qualities of materials. Its asymmetrical compositions, bizarre forms of blooms, foliage, and stems with sinuous flowing lines and mysterious dream-maidens with long wavy hair, known as *femme-fleurs*, spread throughout the architecture and decorative arts of Europe.

In Barcelona, Antonio Gaudi unleashed his visionary imagination to create numerous buildings of amazingly personal designs, culminating in the soaring towers of the Holy Family Church. It has been said of Charles Rennie Mackintosh's work in Scotland that "in our century, no other house has been built that emanates as much poetry as Hill House." Mackintosh also built the famous Glasgow School of Art, a simple, powerful composition free of any form of pomp or pretension that inspired architects in Vienna, another important center of Art Nouveau, and has continued to influence the young architects who study within the Glasgow school's walls today. Among the new art's most important centers were Paris and Brussels, places to which Edouard Empain was intimately connected.

Opposite: Foyer of Victor Horta's
Tassel Hotel in Brussels.

Empain graduated and carried out his business in Brussels, a progressive
and receptive city, as well as a wealthy banking center that became a
magnet for numerous modernist artists. Bourgeois patrons with artistic
and intellectual inclinations were willing to support modern art, and it is
there that the sinuous forms of Art Noveau evolved into what art critics
called the Belgian line. Belgian architect Baron Victor Horta, one of the
most brilliant protagonists of Art Noveau, made his name with the exquisite
Tassel Hotel in Brussels (1893–97), which became a manifesto of the new
style. There, his masterly use of forms emphasized the qualities of different
building materials, and his delicacy of design and clever use of glass and
iron allowed him to achieve a remarkable transparency and lightness.
Numerous other Belgian architects and designers skillfully repeated Horta's
architectural qualities. Although Edouard Empain set up commercial
companies all over the world and, from 1905 to 1914, spent a few months
each year in Egypt, mentally and intellectually he remained in Brussels.

Below: Hector Guimard's decoration of the Paris subway stations.

Opposite: Ever since 1889, the Eiffel Tower and the spirit of the époque in which it was built have been seen as the essence of Paris.

In Paris, Empain was involved in the construction of the Métropolitain subway, a project so inextricably connected with Art Noveau that art historians have called the movement 'Le Style Métro.' Paris Métro company president Adrien Bénard, though as staunchly bourgeois as Empain, had the vision to choose one of the new and contesting artists, Hector Guimard, to design the metro's surface structures and surroundings and, despite early strong criticism from the public, to see to it that his designs were carried out. Guimard's flowing, organic forms, colored green and featuring phantasmagoric vegetal shapes as decoration, were shocking to the conservative critics of the time, but soon became the darling of the French public, icons of Art Noveau, and, in a way, a symbol of Paris itself. We do not know if Empain ever met Guimard, or if he was involved in making decisions about the design, but certainly he was intimately familiar with Le Style Métro.

Another important aspect of European architecture in 1900 was the search for national styles. In spite of their generally classical inspiration, mainstream buildings in the academic style tended to put on regional costumes, imitating Renaissance palazzos in Italy, the Versailles in miniature in France, or Tudor country manors in England. Countries under foreign domination or occupation, such as Poland, Hungary, or Finland looked to architecture to express their national identities.

The new designs coexisted with ancient monuments in old cities to form the European architecture that Edouard Empain knew. We can imagine Empain in Paris in 1900 as he walks into the grounds of the largest and most splendid World Exhibition ever and under the giant arch "Electricity" that had been decorated with three thousand colored lamp bulbs, then still a novelty. He then wanders past the neo-baroque opulence of the Grand Palais and Petit Palais and the numerous exhibition halls. Later, outside the exhibition grounds, he boards one of the electric-powered subway trains that swiftly transport people through the extensive city of grand buildings and spacious boulevards via stations flowering with the imaginative forms of the new, free style.

It was Belle Époque at its height, and Edouard Empain belonged to the small group who were wealthy enough to fully enjoy the sweeping modernization, increasing prosperity, dazzling society life, and flourishing arts. Perhaps he was planning how to set up his huge electric companies as he watched the spectacle of colored lamps. Soon he would be planning a city.

Although the future Baron chose architects well-acquainted with the new European trends to build his city, the original Heliopolis buildings didn't follow these trends. It's true they used the contrast between huge surfaces of blank walls and judiciously placed architectural details as their main means of architectural expression. In this, their design owes much to the new architecture of Vienna, Glasgow, or Barcelona. However, their style cannot be termed Art Nouveau. It was not in the forms of particular buildings, but in the urban design where Empain's creation followed the most modern trends of its times.

Opposite: Buildings on Ibrahim al-Laqqani Street (formerly Boulevard Abbas.)

The name Heliopolis comes from the Greek. Yet the modern city was created in times far removed from the era when the Greek *polis* was the model of a Mediterranean city, both in its architecture and urban spaces, and in its social organization. With the industrialization of the nineteenth century, important European cities developed into giant metropolitan centers, offering wealth, economic opportunities, variety, and change. There were negative aspects to this development, however: overpopulation, congestion, unsanitary living conditions, pollution, and lack of green areas and places for recreation. By the end of the nineteenth century, many Europeans felt the time was ripe for changes in the way cities were planned and how they functioned.

In England, Sir Ebenezer Howard, inspired by the Utopian ideal of cooperative ventures to achieve social reform, proposed a visionary solution for curing the ills of densely populated modern cities. People should be provided with an environment that combined the best of town living and country living. This he referred to as a 'garden city': a community of limited size and low-density housing built in the green countryside, but complete with important services, jobs, and cultural amenities for its inhabitants. Howard's vision remained largely a dream. Instead, dormitory suburbs sprawled around the big cities. But at the time when Edouard Empain planned Heliopolis, the idea was still hot. Howard presented his scheme in the book *Tomorrow: a Peaceful Way to Real Reform* published in 1898, and the Garden Cities Association was formed in 1899. The book was re-published in 1902 as *Garden Cities of Tomorrow*, and the first model city at Letchworth in Hertfordshire was begun in 1903. A number of similar experiments soon followed in Germany and in Belgium.

Empain didn't intend to create a garden city along Howard's lines. His enterprise probably had more in common with the project that first used the name: Garden City on Long Island, in Nassau County, southern New York State. There, in 1869, a wealthy New York merchant Alexander T. Stewart bought 7,000 acres of land that he developed into a model city with parks and wide tree-lined avenues. Nonetheless, Empain, though not interested in utopian social reform, was no doubt influenced by the much-discussed concept of the garden city when he decided to create a satellite town near Cairo, and there are clear similarities between the plans of Heliopolis and Letchworth. After all, Howard's book was concerned mostly with the economic aspects of the Garden City, and argued convincingly

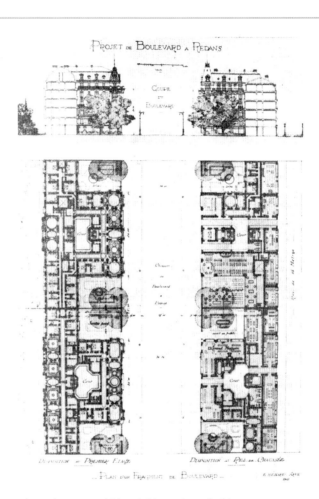

that such a scheme could be viable and profitable.

Heliopolis also followed the modern urban planning trends of its time on another level. The design of its buildings, regardless of the appearance of their façades, reflected the ideas that preoccupied contemporary architects and planners.

The houses that emerged after the industrial revolution in formerly medieval European cities typically featured a drive-through gateway into a courtyard, with the prime apartments located in the front wing that faced a street. Second-class apartments and the service areas of the front apartments were located in the side and back wings, with their windows overlooking the courtyard. The builders were responding to market forces, leading to a highly standardized design quite independent of the style of the front façade. Plots of land were tailored by developers for the needs of precisely this kind of building. By the end of the nineteenth century, the

Opposite and below: Designs for "Boulevard á Redans" by Eugène Hénard, published in 1903 in the journal *L'Architecture*, were one of the various solutions proposed at the time as alternatives to the then-prevalent urban planning.

cost-cutting and revenue seemed to have been perfected to the last detail; nothing more could be earned within the standardized design.

In a fiercely competitive market, architects were soon pressed to produce new designs to squeeze in even more value. Shops, which yielded high rents, were given a second level on mezzanines. Electric-powered elevators made it possible to create luxury flats on all floors. Previously, the more stairs a tenant had to climb the less valuable the apartment would be. By about 1900, builders were working all out to increase the number of high-rent apartments and decrease the number of low-rent apartments on any given plot. One clever solution was to combine several standard-sized lots where apartments would have been built around courtyards not much bigger than light-shafts into a single large lot where the windows of apartments opened onto a common space that could be planted with greenery: a luxury in the crowded industrial cities. (This was a creative adaptation of concepts that had been present in European urban planning before, in such developments as the Place des Vosges or Place Dauphine in Paris, and in British housing around common green squares.)

Above: The façade of a residential building on Ibrahim al-Laqqani Street (formerly Boulevard Abbas) stretches for close to a hundred meters.

Opposite: Arcaded balconies of a residential building overlooking front gardens.

For Heliopolis, where inexpensive desert acreage was abundant, Empain was not pressed to cram full every square foot of his land. But it was crucial for him to attract a well-paying clientele. His architects therefore followed the modern trend when they created buildings containing only luxury apartments, often with the extra indulgence of small, private gardens opening off ground floor units. Heliopolis's first apartment buildings stand on lots much longer than the standard twenty or twenty-two meters used in European cities (as well as downtown Cairo and Alexandria), and as a result their monumental façades are many times as long. This gave the buildings a palatial aspect attractive to well-to-do clientele. Some of the early buildings were spacious apartment blocks arranged around huge common courtyards, and were entered from small pedestrian streets running between gardens, therefore offering greenery and privacy even though the houses were prestigiously located on a main street. This was just the kind of design that was discussed in the progressive European architectural journals of the day.

③ OASIS D'HELIOPOLIS.

MAISONS MUSULMANES AVEC ÉTAGE.

TYPE MUS. AGRANDI-

FAÇADES.

ÉCHELLE, DE 0.02. p.m.

N.B. Les côtés sont a suivre —

A special area of the new city was designated to house service workers and servants. Their lodgings were economical and utilitarian, yet designed to allow them to live in dignity, in sound, hygienic living conditions. In this, the designers of Heliopolis were at the forefront of the "social architecture" that was hotly discussed among progressive architects in Europe. They were thus forerunners of the radical modernist trends that surfaced with clamorous force after the First World War. Yet, unlike the modernists of the years to come, the designers of Heliopolis never felt that functional architecture must be devoid of embellishment. It was still two decades before architecture would embrace Mies van der Rohe's slogan "less is more"; Baron Empain's architects would probably have subscribed to Robert Venturi's response in the 1980s, "less is a bore."

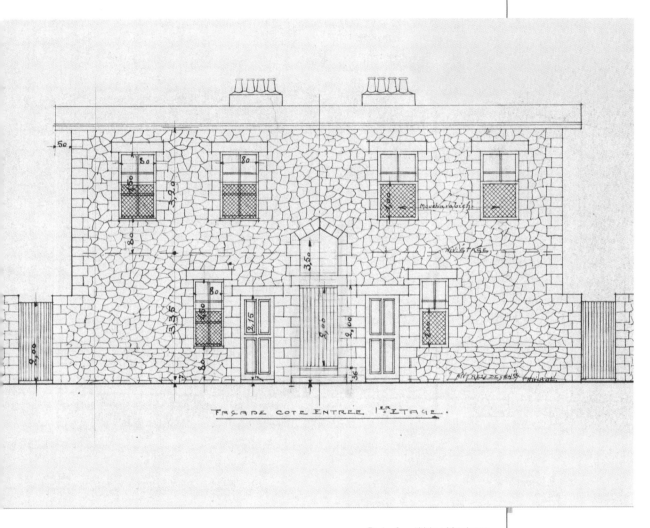

Design for a "Maison Musulmane
Agrandi" from the Heliopolis
Company's early days.

The Heliopolis Company's
headquarters and the buildings
at the corner of Boulevard Abbas
and Boulevard Isma'il
photographed in the 1920s from
the Heliopolis Palace Hotel.

THE ART OF CITY MAKING

Building a new city requires the concerted effort of many people, and Edouard Empain had a talent for hiring the right architects, engineers, builders, and administrators. One person he did not need was someone to provide him with a clear overall vision: he had it himself. Yet his vision wasn't fixed and static. His Heliopolis project adapted to changing circumstances.

An engineer, Empain decided his own company was best qualified to provide the all-important infrastructure for the City of the Sun. The company bored hundred-meter-deep artesian wells in 1907 and built two huge reservoirs in which to store water. It built a power plant at Shubra al-Khaima close to the Nile which, from 1912, provided electricity to Heliopolis residents at prices slightly below those in Cairo. The company was rather less successful, however, in providing a third service: sewage disposal. To the east of the new city it built bacterial plants with sewage farms and septic tanks and planted two rows of eucalyptus trees around the tanks to hide the unpleasant site from public view. But it could not hide the smell. Two or three times a week, the septic tanks had to be cleaned, sending nefarious odors that wafted across the new city. As the population grew and the sewage increased, temporary filtration ponds were constructed, only to breed massive swarms of mosquitoes and cause pools of salty wastewater to form along the road to al-Qubba, to the northwest. This was quite a disincentive to potential homebuyers. The situation stank. To resolve the problem, the company in the end had to give up some of its autonomy. After negotiations, it arranged for the extension of a large government sewage line in 1909 to connect Heliopolis to the Cairo sewage system.

The Hippodrome, in the place
now occupied by the Merryland
park.

There were other troubles too. In 1907 an economic crisis hit Egypt, and plots in Heliopolis did not sell well. The company, falling back on its huge resources, managed to keep investing, while hoping that sales would rebound when the economy improved. It surveyed forty kilometers of avenues and streets, then built, paved, and planted them with trees. A tramway line connected Heliopolis to downtown Cairo in 1908 and another to the upscale district of Abbasiya in 1909. With a few hundred lodgings already built, the company began developing a race track, an aerodrome, the Luna Park amusement center, and other public spaces to attract a European clientele and increase the land's value. It spared no effort in providing modern public services, including telephone connections, a police station, a medical first-aid service and, already by 1910, two post offices. To the same purpose, it encouraged religious and other organizations

97

to provide places of worship and schools by offering land and even buildings for free or a token fee.

Then, just when it seemed sales were set to take off, the First World War broke out. It was only after the war and a string of nationalist uprisings in Egypt in 1919 had ended that the city was able to emerge triumphant and to function as a real urban organism. By that time, buildings and streets had been constructed, infrastructure was in place, and social, educational, and cultural needs were provided for. People began moving in en masse.

The twenty-five square kilometer tract that the company bought from the Egyptian government was, in 1906, roughly the same size as the whole of Cairo itself. Initially, Empain envisaged developing two 'oases' on parcels of land that represented only a small fraction of the whole, both surrounded by natural desert landscape. One of these, some 2 kilometers by 1.5 kilometers (roughly 740 acres), was the nucleus of modern Heliopolis, and in fact the original name for the city was 'The Oasis of Heliopolis.' To this day this area remains the unquestionable center of the district, which by now, however, has devoured any piece of desert for miles around and has merged with Cairo in a continuous urban agglomeration. The second oasis, planned for Almaza, to the southeast of Heliopolis, never materialized. Rather, most new development followed a corridor to the northeast that had deliberately been left open. The city's expansion in other directions was blocked by man-made boundaries of tramway tracks, industrial installations, and, later, recreational facilities.

There are still places in Heliopolis that feel like an oasis.

Opposite: View from the greenery of the garden in the Basilica (formerly Queen Elisabeth) Square on the corner of Harun al-Rashid Street (formerly Avenue San Stefano).

Above: Roxy Square, formerly the site of the Luna Park amusement center.

Above: The Notre Dame Basilica
designed by Alexandre Marcel
and built in 1911–13.

Opposite: Aerial view of Queen
Elisabeth Square and the Basilica
in 1940s.

One can feel the influence of Haussmann's Paris in the plan of Heliopolis: grand avenues, spacious city squares linked by wide streets or arching boulevards, and a range of landmark buildings carefully placed to impose grand views on the cityscape. Far from being a rustic retreat or a company town of regimented housing, Heliopolis was meant to be a true city. The monumental Avenue of the Pyramids (today Al-Ahram Street), clearly intended as an equivalent of the Champs Elysées *(tous les proportions gardeés)*, ends at the city's main square, christened Queen Elisabeth Square in honor of Belgian King Albert I's wife, where towers the dome of a Roman Catholic basilica.

On the other side of the square, the street forks diagonally into two: Tanta Street and Muhammad 'Ali Street (nowadays 'Uthman Ibn 'Affan and Harun al-Rashid). Another major boulevard crosses the square perpendicularly. The avenues span widths of thirty to forty meters and the main streets twenty to twenty-five meters. The square—with its five streets spoking out to form a star, or *étoile*, with the wide façades that flanked its edges so allowing long perspectives onto the streets, and with its spacious gardens on either side—was designed to look truly magnificent. The Place de l'Opéra in Paris immediately comes to mind, but the monumental edifice that stands in the middle of the square is of a different kind.

Here, in the central and the most important place in the city, the Basilica stands as a message from Baron Empain, a Roman Catholic himself: this luxury city is built for people like me. The building is an odd compromise between the Christian tradition, the oriental costume of the city, and Art Nouveau architecture. It is modern for its time in its simple, bold design and, with its grand porch of monolithic columns of polished granite and a huge spherical dome, is undeniably impressive. Yet it is not to everyone's taste. Evocative of the Haghia Sophia in Constantinople, it looks strangely non-Latin for a Roman Catholic church and incongruous with the neo-Islamic forms of the buildings around it.

The square measures 190 by 250 meters, eight times the size of a football field, and is mostly covered by greenery. The early plans for Heliopolis seem to indicate that it was initially planned to be of a much smaller scale, and it seems that the original design was modified as a result of the 1907 crisis, when the company realized the new city needed both grandeur and ample green spaces to attract customers.

Behind the Basilica, on the northern side of the square, two large residential buildings formed the backdrop to the church when viewed from the Avenue of the Pyramids. Each featured an imitation minaret with an Ottoman-period top. The faux minarets were never intended for the call to prayer, or even to decorate the structures to which they are attached, but rather to form a part of the city landscape. Indeed, they look awkward in the context of just a single building; they make aesthetic sense only by their flanking of the streets that branch off Basilica Square.

Opposite and below:
The northeastern side of Basilica
Square, marking the division
between the "European" and the
"Oriental" parts of Heliopolis.

The architect clearly intended to avoid the rigid formality that would result from putting two towers on either ends of one building—a solution that would have also been contrary to how real Ottoman minarets in Cairo were placed. Instead, Baron Empain preferred two asymmetrical, picturesque buildings that combined into a symmetrical urban composition.

The two towers, disproportionately tall compared to the buildings they adorned, stood on a dividing line: to the west was the 'European city' of palaces, villas, and luxury flats and, to the east, where Heliopolis's principal mosque was also located, lay the cheaper housing, including the 'indigenous quarters.' Were the towers intended as a visual indication of where the 'native' city began? Or were they simply picturesque devices to enliven the new city's silhouette and make it fit to be a part of Cairo, the 'City of a Thousand Minarets?' (They were not the only fake minarets in Heliopolis.) Whatever the architect's motives, on an urban scale they form

Opposite: One of the faux
minarets on the northeastern side
of Basilica Square, its top missing
after the 1992 earthquake.

Below: The porch of the Basilica.

a fine defining element in the square's composition, complementing and
counterbalancing the Basilica that stands in its middle. The faux minarets
lost their tops after the 1992 earthquake. Did they become structurally
unstable? Or were they removed because it was felt they inappropriately
imitated architectural elements reserved for religious purposes?

Even though the early-twentieth-century urban designers would have
had no inkling of the density of today's Cairo traffic, the sheer grandeur
of the design almost always prevents the overwhelming volume of
automobiles from clogging these arteries. Still, the traffic, the modern
tramway line that runs through the square, the asphalt encircling the few
desolate-looking lawns, and the fences that close off the two beautifully
kept gardens have destroyed some of the Basilica square's former splendor.
Today the space is vast and empty, difficult to cross without a hat on
summer days. Yet even now, at night it is busy with families picnicking on
patches of grass, and neighborhood boys often play football there. Every
Sunday, the square comes alive with the elegant crowd that gathers in
front of the church for the service. With their diamonds sparkling and fur
coats shining, it's easy to imagine similar scenes in the shadow of the
Basilica's grand porch a century earlier.

Above: Baghdad Street, formerly Boulevard Isma'il.

Opposite: Ibrahim al-Laqqani Street, formerly Boulevard Abbas.

Following pages: Some of Heliopolis's surviving greenery: balconies facing front gardens in an alley off Ibrahim al-Laqqani Street; Roxy Square.

The Avenue of the Pyramids, the two main diagonal streets that join in a 'Y' at the main square, and the perpendicular avenue that leads to the Baron's own palace form Heliopolis's simple, symmetrical framework: these were enclosed on three sides by circular boulevards and tramway tracks, while smaller streets and alleys filled the space in between. Even though Heliopolis was a brand new city laid out in the open desert, it didn't employ a soulless rectangular grid. Nor did it exploit picturesque fancies of fake rural landscapes with curving streets and irregular lots. Rather, it attempted—quite successfully—to achieve variety and richness by turning landmarks such as the Basilica, the Heliopolis Palace Hotel, the Baron's palace, the main mosque, and other monumental buildings into focal points connected by wide and spacious avenues to create grand vistas. Again, Paris instantly comes to mind.

Heliopolis was truly meant to be an oasis in the desert. Eight percent of the area was designated for public gardens, parks, and playgrounds, and already in 1906 a plan for gardens was laid out. No more than fifty percent of any private lot could be built up, and many of the villas and palaces stood in huge gardens. To the south, behind the Palace Hotel, which had its own large garden, extended the Heliopolis Sporting Club with its golf course, and to the north was the race track.

Creating a garden in the desert was a difficult task; it meant bringing not only water, but also soil. Recycled water from the Shubra power plant was piped to Heliopolis and used for watering the gardens. Fertile Nile soil was brought first by horse cart, then later by truck. In 1907, one of the customers who had planned building a palace in Heliopolis annulled his contract stating, "I would never like to live alone in the desert." Yet, by 1915, the place was no longer desert, but a veritable oasis, a true garden city, with greenery in every neighborhood. Date palms, hibiscus, agaves, geraniums, and jacarandas graced the Avenue of the Pyramids. The tree-lined boulevards were advertised as the Champs Elysées of Cairo. To promote sales, the Heliopolis Company organized numerous feasts and events to encourage Cairenes to visit and enjoy the green areas. Still, the desert was not forgotten. Baron Empain, himself much in love with the desert, advertised his enterprise as a desert adventure and the Heliopolis Palace Hotel as "Sahara Palace."

Above: Avenue of the Pyramids,

Opposite: A villa on Nazih Khalifa Street (formerly Avenue Baron Empain). Although the original Heliopolis's rather strict spatial divisions between different social strata have often been blurred, some parts of the district retain their exclusive character.

The simple framework of avenues and boulevards served the different needs of different types of inhabitants without the divisions being immediately visible in the city's general layout. The zoning was nevertheless quite strict. Hotels, clubs, and sporting facilities were located on the southern fringes of the town, while a number of industrial installations were confined to the outskirts in the north. The most sumptuous villas and palaces, among them the Baron's, were located to the south, beyond the circular boulevards and close to the desert. The company constructed huge apartment buildings with spacious rental flats along the main streets in the city's core. The area north of the Basilica contained houses for the working class, also mostly company-built. The rest of the land was divided into standard-sized lots, averaging twenty meters by thirty-three meters. Those in the southern areas sported villas surrounded by gardens and recessed far from the streets, while those in the central area contained apartment buildings or villas that stood close to the streets.

The Heliopolis enterprise used up-to-date European building technology, not in pursuit of any architectural ideals, but rather to keep costs down. Heliopolis was grand, but never wasteful. In the project's initial phase, almost all building materials, even bricks, were imported, mostly from Belgium and France. The years of hardship after the 1907 economic crisis, however, forced the company to rely on local materials.

Much of Heliopolis was built of calcium silicate brick, an unburned brick made of sand and hydrated lime. The off-white bricks were produced at the company's own plant in Heliopolis's northern outskirts using inexpensive local materials. The company also often employed rough stone masonry, which enabled it to draw on the talents of less costly local masons. It not only used reinforced concrete—still a novelty at the time—for columns and lintels, but also for balconies, terraces, and floor slabs, a practice that put Heliopolis at the forefront of modern building technology. This rational, utilitarian aspect of the city's architecture is particularly visible in the lower-class lodgings and in the back elevations of more prestigious buildings.

Opposite: The back side of a
luxurious apartment building off
Ibrahim al-Laqqani Street.

Below: Peeling plaster reveals the
building techniques used in
Heliopolis in 1910s. Calcium
silicate bricks reinforce the corner
of a rough stone masonry wall;
the edge of a concrete floor slab
is exposed.

The front façades concealed the practicalities of construction under a veneer of high-quality plaster. The decorative details were also made of plaster (or, if structurally necessary, concrete), pre-cast, and attached to the walls. The plaster casting used a sophisticated technology, with one mix for the substrate layer and another for the fine outer details and moldings, which enabled the company to benefit from economies of scale. Unlike this fake detailing that imitated historic stone-cut pieces, the columns that formed the arcades along the main streets were structural, not decorative. The imposing, monolithic pieces of Aswan granite, polished to a luster, are among Heliopolis' most impressive features, especially nowadays, when virtually nothing in Egypt is built of stone and the use of Aswan granite, once the pride of monumental edifices, is confined to thinly sliced cladding.

Opposite: Neo-Mamluk decoration in cement plaster on the front façade of a building on Baghdad Street.

Above: Granite columns of a building on the same street.

Opposite: A huge, palatial villa built for Boghos Nubar Pasha on Avenue Generale Baron Empain, now Nazih Khalifa Street.

The company's architectural office in Brussels and its Cairo branch were charged with enforcing the regulations laid out for the buildings. No more than half of the standard lots could be built upon and only one-third of a lot in the prime villas area. A minimum height for each floor was set. Buildings lining the streets had to fill the entire width of their lots and their height had to be no more than one-and-a-half times the width of the street, and no taller then five stories. The height of villas could not exceed fifteen meters. Similarly strict rules governed sanitary infrastructure and room ventilation.

The company offered four categories of lodging to match different incomes and lifestyles: villas, bourgeois flats in apartment buildings, small apartments in blocks of flats (which the company called 'garden-cities') and, finally, austere bungalows for the working class. Within each category were further sub-divisions, such as villas with a dome, villas with a tower, and so on.

The villas ranged in size from 130 to 300 square meters and contained all the accessories of a well-to-do life: entrance halls with wardrobes, living rooms, dining and drawing rooms, libraries, covered terraces, huge kitchens, and living quarters for servants. The more sumptuous homes would feature a domed central grand hall, often a cellar, and always a *WC arabe* for servants, located by the outer fence. Some of the buildings along the boundary that separated areas designated for apartment buildings from those designated for villas (such as the building at 14 Baron Street, which has housed the Polish Archaeological Center since the 1950s) were designed either to be used as a huge single-family house or to be divided, with one apartment on each floor.

Below: An apartment building on Baghdad Street, formerly Boulevard Isma'il.

Opposite: The balcony of a residential building off Ibrahim al-Laqqani Street, formerly Boulevard Abbas.

The apartment buildings designed for the bourgeoisie usually consisted of six or eight apartments conforming to the European 'post-Haussmann' pattern for rented flats. Each apartment comprised an entrance hall, living and dining rooms, two to four bedrooms, and a terrace or balcony. Servants had a separate entrance, but not a separate staircase as was the case in similar homes in Europe. Although the apartments were fairly big, from seventy to 150 square meters, they, in common with their European contemporaries, had only a single bathroom.

119

The 'garden cities' consisted of buildings with small apartments of thirty-three to sixty-nine square meters, which typically comprised two bedrooms, a living room, kitchen, and bathroom. Apartments on the ground floor opened onto small gardens, while those on the upper floors had loggias. The apartments were often entered from open galleries along the back side of the building.

The lowest category of lodging was of two types: bungalows for the workmen and the units of the "indigenous quarters," as the Company named the lowest-standard dwellings. A bungalow had two rooms, a kitchen, and a miniature garden of about sixteen square meters, with the sanitary facilities placed in the garden. In the "indigenous city," twenty-four living units were placed together in blocks on either side of a six-meter-wide street. Each unit had two rooms that opened onto a walled six-by-seven-meter courtyard, entered from the street. In the corners of the courtyard were a cooking oven and an "indigenous toilet." The rooms were only 3.3 meters high, and the courtyards were fenced off with 2.5-meter walls.

Opposite: An alley off Harun al-Rashid Street, formerly Rue San Stefano.

Below: Damascus Street (formerly Boulevard Tawfiq) links the luxurious quarters to the market and service areas.

Building #16 Baghdad Street
(formerly Boulevard Isma'il),
designed in 1924 by G. A. Soria
and C. Suares for Sasoon Shohet
and Son.

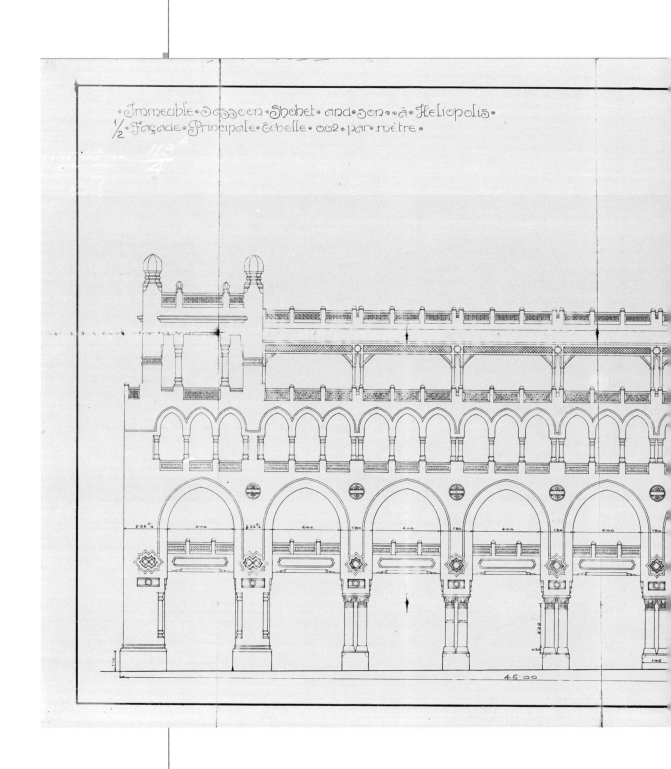

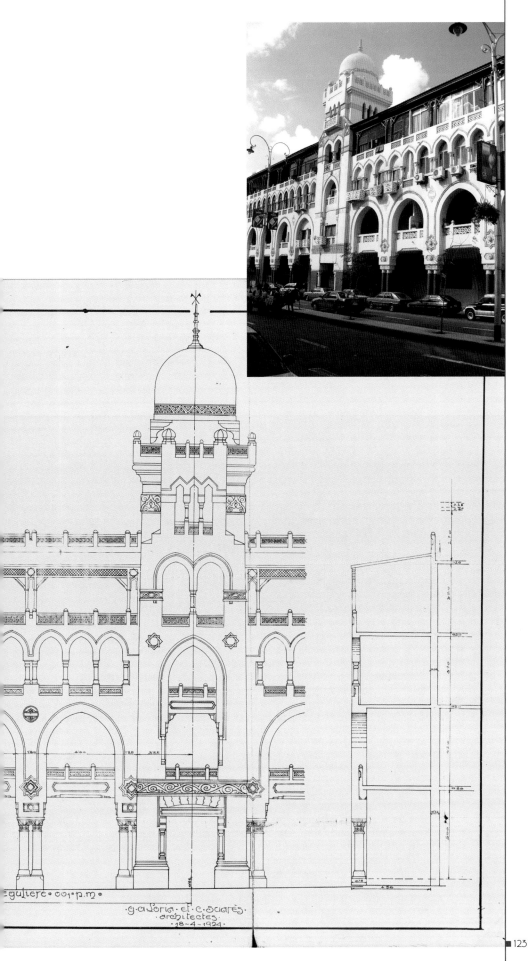

eguliere · ooı · p · m ·

·g·a·Soria· et ·c·Suares·
architectes·
·18–4–1924·

Immeuble de Rapport a Heliopolis
PROPRIETE DE Mᴿ AMIN ABDALLAH
FAÇADE PRINCIPALE
ECHELLE 1:50

Preceding pages: Building #7 on Ibrahim Street, designed in 1932 for Amin Abdallah, drawing signed "Architecte M. I. H. Fahmy, D.R.E.C, A.M.I. Struct. E., London"

Below: Building #2 on Ibrahim al-Laqqani Street (formerly Boulevard Abbas), corner of Roxy Square, designed by Ernest Jaspar in 1909. The drawing bears the stamp "Société Française Enterprises en Egypte, 75 B° Haussmann, Paris".

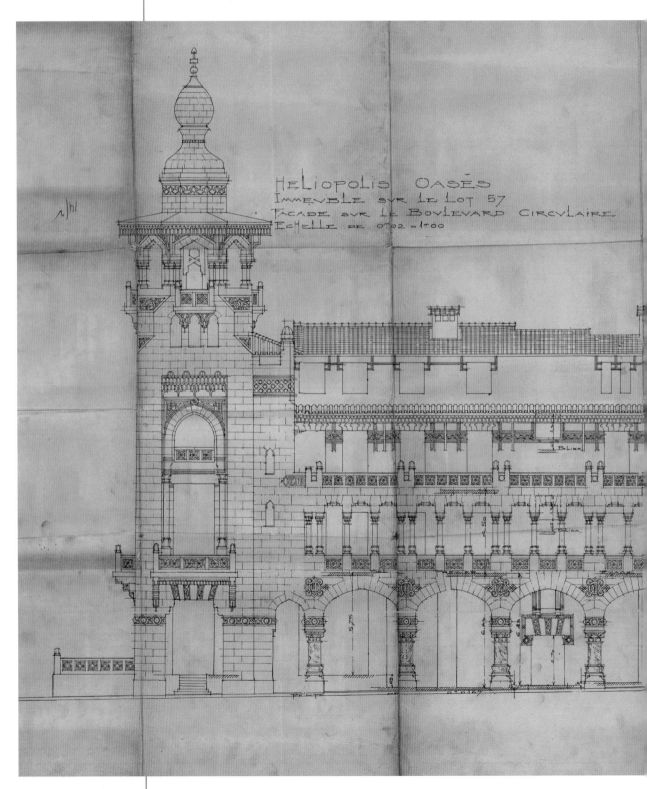

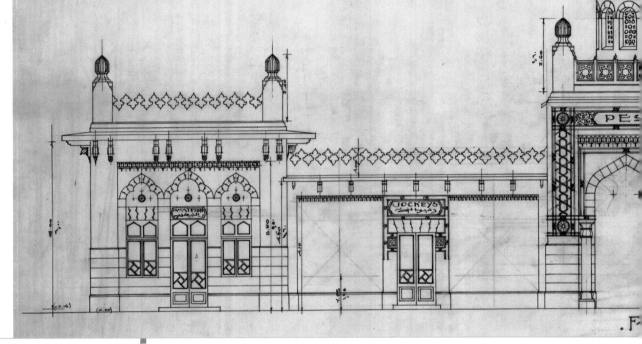

. PLAN N° C.219.

. AMÉNAGEMENTS DU NOUVEAU PADDOCK.

. BÂTIMENT ʿA.
. PAVILLON DU PESAGE.
. ÉCHELLE 2/100.

. N.B. L'ENTREPRENEUR EST TENU DE
VÉRIFIER LES CÔTES.

Design drawing for the scales
pavilion at the Hippodrome,
signed: "Bureau d'Architecture,
Heliopollis".

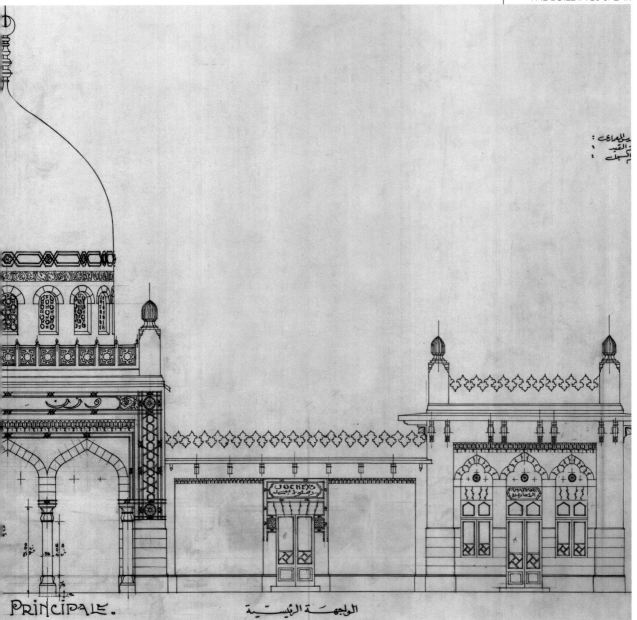

PRINCIPALE. الواجهــــة الرئيســـية

LANDMARKS

Already in 1912, Heliopolis residents enjoyed five schools, an abundance of religious buildings, a sporting club, a hippodrome, a casino, a Luna Park, and an airport. There were two hotels, post offices, a dispensary, and a police station. A number of spectacular palaces enriched the cityscape.

Perhaps the most impressive landmark of all was the Heliopolis Palace Hotel. The result of cooperation between the city's two main architects, Ernest Jaspar and Alexandre Marcel, with Jaspar the chief designer, the hotel had a two-and-a-half-million-dollar budget to ensure its grandeur. It was the biggest hotel in the world, covering 6,500 square meters and containing four hundred rooms—fifty-five of them suites—banqueting halls, lounges, and a huge restaurant. A reinforced concrete dome soared thirty-five meters above its splendid lobby.

"It borrows from the Arab architecture in the most appealing way: flavor of transparency, perspective, and space," raved an art magazine in a 1929 review. Yet the Islamic borrowings, however tasteful and harmonious, constituted mere adornments to a building which, with its immense formal façade, owed its overall concept to Versailles and the École des Beaux Arts. The sumptuous interiors in a variety of styles, furnished with huge mirrors, oriental carpets, marble columns, and mahogany furniture imported from London, were designed to make guests feel they were the cream of society. There they enjoyed weddings and honeymoons, met for tea after races or a visit to the nearby sporting club—or just dined royally on the culinary creations of Chef Gouin, who had been brought from Paris. The Belgian king Albert II was perhaps the hotel's most eminent guest. He stayed for an entire month in 1911 after a doctor recommended the dry climate of Heliopolis for his wife, who was recuperating from an illness.

When the First World War broke out, the British turned the hotel into a military hospital and later, for a time, an aviation school. After the Second World War, cheaper hotels began stealing its custom, and the ouster of the monarchy in Egypt in 1952 dampened the social life of the old days. By the 1960s, the hotel, a remnant of a different époque, was neglected and decaying, then finally abandoned. In the 1980s it was renovated and turned into administrative premises of the President of Egypt.

The Heliopolis Palace Hotel in the 1920s or 1930s.

Below: The front façade facing Boulevard Abbas (now Ibrahim al-Laqqani Street).

Opposite: The *Salon de jeu et de repos.*

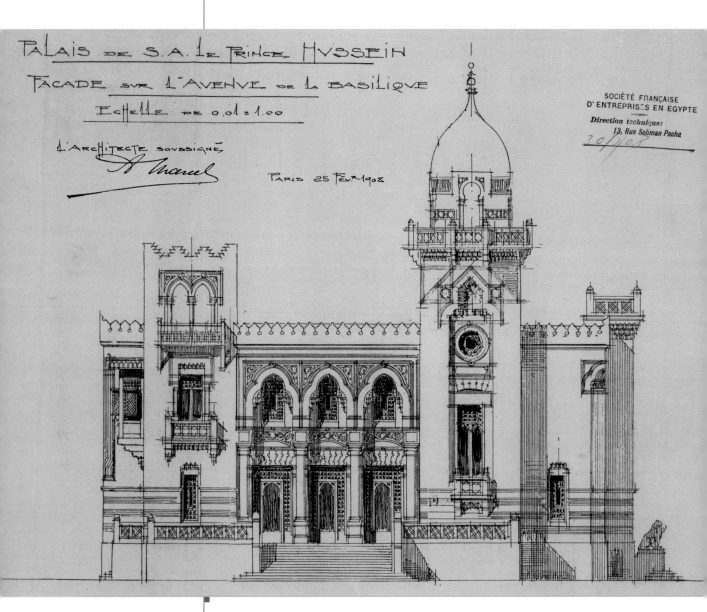

Above and opposite: Architectural design drawings for the palace of Prince (later Sultan) Hussein Kamel; by Alexandre Marcel, 1908. The plan to the right shows that the Prince ordered the architect to alter the plan slightly to make the palace larger and even more sumptuous.

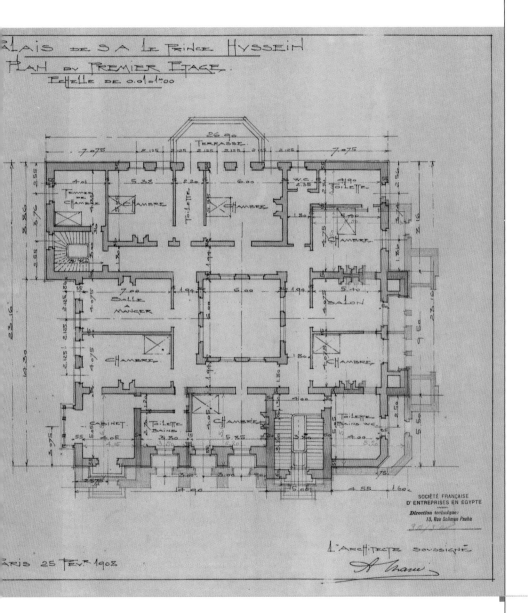

Among other landmarks of Heliopolis were the palaces. Sultan Hussein Kamel's sported decorative recesses that ran through the whole height of the building, crenellations, and a centrally located dome, making it look more like a mosque than a Mamluk palace. The Sultan, who reigned in 1914–17, was, along with President Muhammad Hosni Mubarak, one of two Egyptian rulers to reside in modern Heliopolis. The forty-room palace of his wife Sultana Malak also had an Islamic touch. Like the rest of residential architecture in Heliopolis, however, the palaces were quite European in plan and spatial arrangement, wearing only the costume of Islamic architecture.

Baron Empain built his own palace in a completely different style—a Hindu temple fantasy in reinforced concrete. When it was constructed in 1907–10, it overlooked the desert, and the Baron is said to have enjoyed gazing at the pyramids from its terrace. With so many stories circulating about the building, however, it's hard to decide which to believe. Yet, in the days long before Cairo sprouted skyscrapers and gained a curtain of smog, this one at least seems plausible. Among the guests was the Belgian king Albert I. In the following years the Empain family continued to host banquets and parties for two generations more, until it sold the palace and its sumptuous garden in 1956. The buyers were Syrian and Saudi business partners who for years tried to turn it into a hotel or a casino, but never obtained a permit from the Egyptian authorities. The building deteriorated and the garden died, until the Ministry of Housing, after seemingly endless negotiations with innumerable inheritors, acquired it in 2005. A rehabilitation project has been launched to open to the public a landmark palace that anybody going to or from the Cairo airport is almost certain to notice.

Preceding pages: Baron Empain's palace, designed by Alexandre Marcel in 1911.

Below and opposite: Two of the earliest Heliopolitan buildings from before the First World war, both on Ibrahim al-Laqqani Street (formerly Boulevard Abbas).

COSTUMES OF THE ORIENT

The streets of Heliopolis reflected a contemporary European urban lifestyle, and the houses that lined them, apart from the most basic ones, were laid out on a European model. And yet Edouard Empain decided the new city's appearance should be Islamic. On a personal level, he was fascinated with the desert and probably drawn by the Orient's lure. Yet perhaps a more important consideration was that the style should appeal to buyers and tenants. In a project as risky as his, he must have looked for an uncontroversial and safe option; the public was used to buildings clad in historical costume, and an "oriental" one certainly seemed appropriate.

Façade Principale.

Such a costume, though exotic, was not unfamiliar to Europe. The popular and prolific orientalist artists had long romanticized and re-interpreted the Orient, and at the grand industrial exhibitions, including the splendid 1900 exhibition in Paris, "Oriental" or "Mauresque" pavilions abounded. Empain must have visited many. At the same time, the idea of "Islamic Revival" architecture was not new to Cairo. Already in the 1820s, Pascal Coste proposed to Muhammad 'Ali that he build his great mosque at the Citadel in a neo-Mamluk style (the Pasha eventually decided to follow models from Istanbul).

By the end of the nineteenth century the ruling family had embraced the Islamic style. "Her Excellency the Khedive's mother, as well as his Excellency the Khedive desired that the building have a grand appearance . . . so Fabricius Bey took as his inspiration the most beautiful monuments of the Arab architecture from its heyday," reads a book commemorating the construction of the Royal Family mausoleum in 1894 in Cairo's Eastern Cemetery. The mausoleum skillfully employed Mamluk architectural and decorative elements in a very formal and regular Beaux Arts building, an architectural arrangement very different from the irregular layouts of medieval Mamluk buildings. The Ministry of Religious Endowments (*Awqaf*) was built in downtown Cairo in 1898 in a similar style, as was the Islamic Museum in 1903–04. Max Hertz, who took over the construction of the Rifa'i Mosque in 1905, finished it in grand neo-Mamluk style.

Opposite: Pascal Coste's proposal for Muhammad 'Ali's mosque at the Citadel, 1827.

Below: Interior of Khedive Tawfiq's mausoleum, designed by Fabricius Bey in 1894.

Earlier 'Islamic Revival' buildings such as the tomb of Sulayman Pasha al-Fransawi, who died in 1860, or the Gezira Palace (now part of the Marriott Hotel), which Max Hertz designed in 1864, were architectural fantasies on a vaguely 'Moorish' theme, with nothing specifically Egyptian about them. The buildings of the late nineteenth and early twentieth centuries, however, used motifs borrowed directly from the rich tradition of Islamic architecture in Cairo. Crucially, the designers were able to draw on the work of the Comité de Conservation des Monuments de l'Art Arabe. The Comité, operating under the auspices of the royal family within the Ministry of Religious Endowments, had studied, catalogued, and surveyed hundreds of Islamic monuments in Cairo since its creation in 1882 and had been promptly publishing its work in French.

The decorative elements on the huge apartment buildings on the main streets of Heliopolis were borrowed from a variety of sources. Some were generic 'oriental' motifs, others merely simple geometric forms not traceable to any particular historic style. But the great majority were taken directly from Cairo: motifs of different periods— Fatimid, Mamluk, and Ottoman—copied faithfully, though mixed together. And although the details were Islamic, none of the Heliopolitan buildings was an attempt at an 'archaeological' reconstruction or re-creation of any historical period. The columns, brackets, balustrades, moldings, and crenellations were just interchangeable pieces within the architectural vocabulary. Ottoman or Mamluk, it is how they were placed on the façade, how their multiplication and repetition created rhythms, and how they related to blank undecorated surfaces that mattered. In this respect, the original architecture of Heliopolis has as much in common with Art Nouveau as with historic Islamic architecture.

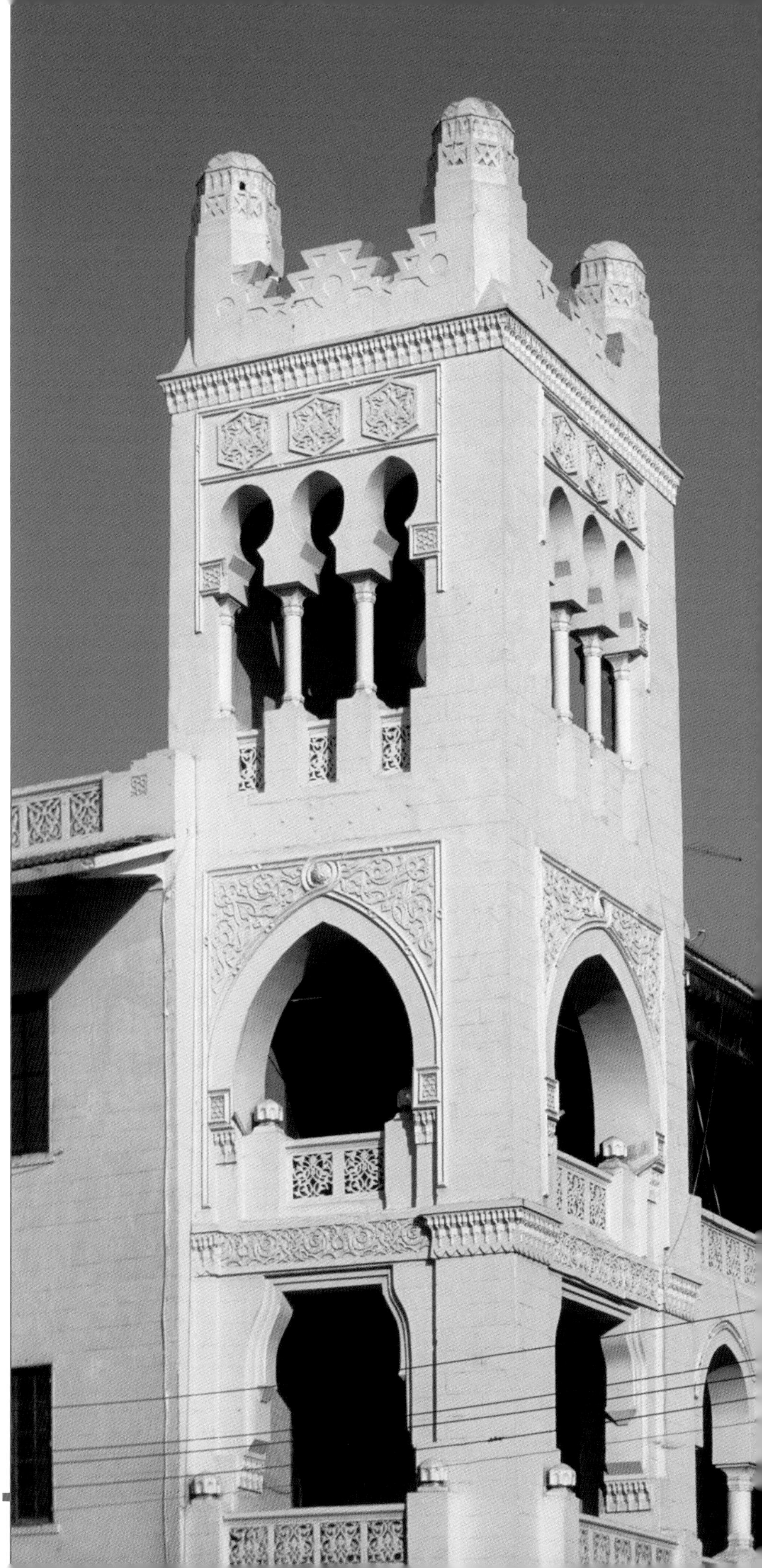

Opposite: Building at the corner
of Ibrahim al-Laqqani and
Baghdad Streets.

Below: Ernest Jaspar, 1876–1940.

Who were the people who created this unique style? One was Ernest Jaspar, the son of a wealthy builder from Brussels who had amassed his fortune from undertaking big urban works for King Leopold II. The younger Jaspar began his studies in 1893 at the Académie des Beaux-Arts in Brussels and participated in Ernest Acker's design of the Belgian pavilion at the international exhibition in Paris in 1900. Jaspar had designed three houses in Brussels, built by the family business, before following the advice of Léon Rolin, a Belgian contractor established in Cairo, and setting off on a journey to the East. The journey brought him to the famous Shepheard Hotel in Cairo in 1904, where he met Empain, who at the time was looking for an architect to design Heliopolis and who offered him the job. It was an offer Jaspar could not reject, and in the spring of 1905 the twenty-eight year old architect moved to Cairo with his family to build the Heliopolis Palace Hotel. The contractor assigned the job was none other than the Léon Rolin who had persuaded Jaspar to come to Cairo in the first place.

Jaspar designed most of the important buildings in Heliopolis and is the man most responsible for its distinctive style. Although a number of European architects worked in Cairo at the time, some with the Comité de Conservation des Monuments de l'Art Arabe, Empain preferred to entrust the architecture to Jaspar. Were the locally established architects like Max Hertz too busy? Too expensive? Perhaps Empain preferred to work with a young man who didn't have his own local agenda.

Another architect was Alexandre Marcel, a Frenchman whom Empain commissioned to build the Basilica and some of the smaller palaces and villas—in addition to his own 'maharaja' style palace. Born in Paris in 1860, Marcel graduated from the faculty of architecture at the famous École des Beaux Arts in Paris. There he opened a practice and later was involved in the great exhibition of 1900, where he helped create the Petit Palais. As part of the exhibition's eclectic architectural landscape, a maritime company commissioned him to build a *Panorama-du-Tour-du-Monde* to illustrate the itinerary of its liners en route from France to the Far East. Marcel designed a building decorated with combined architectural elements from around the world: Japanese, Hindu, Portuguese, and Arab. To some critics, this was a little bit too much, but the Belgian king Leopold II liked it so much that soon after the exposition he asked Marcel for a copy of its Japanese tower and a Chinese pavilion for his royal estate at Laeken. The maharaja of Kapurthala in India then asked Marcel, who had by then developed a reputation as a specialist in 'exotic' architecture, to design an immense palace there surrounded by a garden inspired by Versailles.

Preceding pages: The palace of Baron Empain.

Below: One of Habib Ayrout's sons designed a handsome modernist building at #7, Mameluks Street.

Opposite: The 1930s building on Ibrahim al-Laqqani Street is a modernized version of Ernest Jaspar's style.

Between them, Jaspar and Marcel defined the form of Heliopolitan buildings. The contractors, Léon Rolin and especially Habib Ayrout, whose sons were architects, possibly had some say in the designs, particularly those of the lower-class houses. Ayrout is known to have altered some of the 'garden city' buildings by including "salamliks," or rooms where guests could be received without entering the family quarters, to better suit the needs of Muslim inhabitants. But on the whole, it seems that the unmistakable look of the original Heliopolis was the virtual one-man show of Ernest Jaspar, then in his early thirties. How much he depended on Baron Empain's own ideas and advice we will probably never know.

Above: Post–First World War buildings on Isma'iliya Square continued and developed the architectural style of early Heliopolis.

Opposite: Art Deco buildings on Halab Street.

People who bought their own lots could build villas in styles quite different from Jaspar's. Baron Empain's own villa is a prime example. The company valued richness and variety over uniformity.

Soon after the main avenues were built up, economic recession and the European war caused the company to slow down. Within an interlude of just a few short years, the style of Jaspar's original Heliopolis buildings suddenly became antiquated, a part of a bygone era. When construction resumed after the First World War, there was a degree of continuation in the new houses constructed in the city's northern extension, in the Isma'iliya Square area, and in some infill buildings in the original Heliopolis center. These houses, however, had a style distinctive in their own right, and they belong to a different epoch. They were essentially the same in size and general disposition as the earlier ones, with similar arcades and arched terraces, but were now clothed in a more modern art deco costume in its oriental variant. The simplified neo-Islamic style typical of this period of Heliopolitan architecture can also be seen elsewhere around Cairo in such buildings as the Agricultural Society building in the Gezira showground or the Faculty of Engineering of Ain Shams University.

Below: Art Deco details of a building on Butros Ghali Street.

Opposite: Ibrahim al-Laqqani Street (formerly Boulevard Abbas); the Heliopolis Company's headquarters in the background.

Conventional neo-baroque or neo-renaissance façades also became common. Later, good examples of pure art deco decoration abounded, but in this, Heliopolis was no different from the rest of Cairo. Finally, modernist aesthetics in its different shades and variants appeared, then dominated, until buildings of no aesthetics whatsoever took over in the 1970s and 1980s. Signs of a possible improvement have been emerging since the late 1990s, but these belong to an entirely new architectural era. The original Heliopolis, a swan song of the Belle Époque, was a shooting star: a unique, inimitable, one-time phenomenon.

Arcaded balconies of a residential
building off Ibrahim al-Laqqani
Street.

HELIOPOLIS
A HUNDRED
YEARS ON

The architecture of Heliopolis has had its stern critics. In *Modern Egyptian Art* (AUC Press, 2005), Liliane Karnouk wrote, "The neo-Moorish style adapted in Heliopolis originates in a taste for Islamic decorative arts and grandiose scenographic effects, introduced into Egypt by European colonialists and Orientalists. It does not represent any extension or reveal any understanding of traditional architecture in Egypt. Domes and arches, for instance, are added for purely ornamental effect and serve no other function. Private gardens, arcades, and loggias surround the buildings . . . whereas in traditional Islamic architecture they would be enclosed within the buildings."

These are valid points. But are they the whole truth? The fact that the architects of Heliopolis precisely and consciously copied hundreds of architectural details from different periods of Islamic architecture in Cairo to use as decorative motifs indicates they had at least *some* understanding of traditional architecture in Egypt. In addition, anyone who has ever had the pleasure of sipping tea on a spacious terrace shaded by arched arcades in a Heliopolitan building can easily forgive the purely ornamental function of the gracious arches. One may even think back to what John Ruskin said, and reflect that adorning the edifices raised by man so that the sight of them contributes to his mental health, power, and pleasure may well be considered a valid function in architecture.

Above: Colonnaded arcade on
Ibrahim al-Laqqani Street.

Opposite: Neo-Mamluk
decoration.

And finally, while indeed the use of gardens, arcades, and loggias is very different here than in traditional Islamic architecture (as it is in virtually every building erected in Egypt in the twentieth and twenty-first centuries), their careful design greatly contributed to the quality of life of the inhabitants. Constructed before the era of air-conditioning, the buildings had high ceilings and efficient ventilation systems that allowed their occupants to remain comfortable even in mid-summer. It was sufficient to open windows at nighttime to catch the evening breezes, and then, during the day, to close the wooden shutters on windows that received direct sunshine. (Today, however, because of the noise, one cannot open the windows of apartments on busy streets.) To contribute to the comfort, loggias and arcades were cleverly placed to shelter the apartments from the sun in the hottest time of the day, as were the shaded, green areas in front of the windows. (Nowadays, except in the back streets, the front gardens have almost entirely been devoured by sprawling shops.) The forms are different from those of traditional Islamic architecture, but for the designers of the Heliopolitan buildings, climate control in the interiors was no less important. Similarly, the broad avenues of Heliopolis couldn't be further removed from the narrow streets of the traditional districts of historic Cairo, which are hidden from direct sunlight for most of the day. Nevertheless, one can walk comfortably in Heliopolis even on a hot summer day in the shadow of Mr. Jaspar's monumental arcades, always placed on the southern and western sides of the streets. Baron Empain's creation was perhaps politically incorrect, but it is still a pleasing place to live.

THE
PEOPLE
SPEAK

Butros Ghali Street at its junction
with Ibrahim al-Laqqani Street.
The area where the high-rises
stand was originally taken by four
medium-size and three small villas,
each with its garden.

THE PEOPLE SPEAK

The original Heliopolis is now merely one piece of a much larger urban organism, no longer an oasis of greenery in the desert. Yet it is still an oasis—of graceful historic architecture surrounded by a desert of undistinguished modern buildings. The buildings from Baron Empain's times have become rare exceptions among thousands of houses not differing in any way from those anywhere else in Cairo; these now surround the original Heliopolis and creep into its center as more and more old houses and villas are demolished and replaced with modern structures. Likewise, the people who remember the Heliopolis of the old days, for whom Heliopolis means something more than just another place to live, have become a tiny minority among the population of more than 130,000 as more and more outsiders move in. Yet, one still meets them in the streets of Heliopolis.

Below: Mme Jolanda Badra

Opposite: The Heliopolis House Hotel, which houses Groppi, in the early 1960s.

Madame Yolanda Badra, née Tinnawi, has lived in the district for more than seventy years. She was born and raised in Khartoum in Sudan, but her family was originally from Aleppo, and although the members of the large family have been scattered around the world for generations, they continue to think of themselves as Aleppans. Her parents chose to live in Heliopolis when they moved to Cairo in 1934, then rented a succession of ever larger and more prestigious apartments as they became established. When Yolanda married in 1947, she moved to an apartment in a building owned by her brother-in-law on Boulevard Abbas, and she has been living there ever since.

She speaks of her early days in Heliopolis as of a remote haven. The streets were quiet and full of gardens, and the neighbors were cosmopolitan—Italian, Jewish, Armenian, and Maltese. Live-in Sudanese servants took care of everyday chores. Monday was laundry day: two women came and took over the bathroom, boiling white linens in a large kettle on a primus stove on the bathroom floor, then throwing them into the bathtub with a wooden stick. The milkman brought milk every day; the baker delivered European-style bread to the door; fish were delivered every Friday.

In the stylish shops, shop attendants wearing tarbushes and white gloves sold luxury goods imported from Europe. Tailors and hat makers came to their clients' homes to arrange for special gowns and hats. Weddings were special occasions. Armenian women, their craft mastered over generations, patiently embroidered trousseaux, and a week before the wedding the family would proudly display the pieces to visitors.

The social life was different, too. In the days blissfully without television, people met more often, frequently organizing dinner parties and tea parties, or just gathering for a chat. Food was often catered, and the most coveted caterer was Groppi. Located on the ground floor of the Heliopolis House Hotel at the corner of its namesake Hotel Street and the Avenue des Pyramides, Groppi provided mouthwatering cold cuts and pastries. Today, the restaurant is still at the same location and remains popular, although the coffee is lukewarm and the pastries now greasy and over-sweet.

Below: A postcard of Boulevard Abbas sent to Paris in the 1920s.

Opposite: the dining room of the Heliopolis Palace Hotel.

Sundays were for socializing and entertainment. People went to the movies, with open-air cinemas the most popular. To be seen at the Heliopolis Palace Hotel was a must: Sunday tea parties in winter, music and dancing on summer nights, barbecues in the garden, and nightclubs.

Heliopolitans cherished the esprit of festival, with Christmas and Easter setting the rhythm for the yearly celebrations. In the multinational milieu, the Eastern Christians who celebrated Christmas on 7 January were as numerous as those who ate Christmas dinner on 25 December. In the spirit of compromise, the peak of the celebrations became 1 January, with the shops decorated with frosty landscapes and the occasional animated Santa Claus. Merriment filled the air. Easter was, as now, even more diversified among the different denominations than Christmas. A relic of ancient Egyptian tradition, the springtime feast of Sham-al-Nessim, falling on the day after Orthodox Easter, provided Muslims and Christians alike with an occasion to celebrate.

Yolanda remembers the ups and downs of Heliopolis and of the building in which she has lived for so long. Each apartment had its room on the roof where the servants lived. After the revolution, the roof dwellers in increasing numbers stopped working as servants and became mere squatters, with ever-growing families. Their presence became more and more taxing to the old-time tenants. Eventually, in the wake of a strong earthquake that struck Cairo in 1992, the authorities moved them all to houses in Madinat al-Salam and demolished the roof-top quarters.

Yolanda's daughter Magda remembers how, as a child, she and other children would watch for the occasional car on Boulevard Abbas and bet on the direction from which the next would come. Today, the street teems with cars and noisy crowds of people. She and her mother, however, can still enjoy breakfast and tea on a quiet, spacious terrace on the other side of the building that faces a garden shaded by old mango trees.

Hanim Sadek's apartment is of the same size and layout as Yolanda's. The entry, however, is from a different pedestrian alley through another garden. Both kitchen balconies, where their laundry—now washed by machines, rather than washwomen—dries on clotheslines, face the same immense backyard. Hanim comes from Germany, where her family lost everything in the Allied bombing of Leipzig in 1945. After a strenuous journey through devastated Europe, she arrived in Egypt with her German mother and her father, who was of Nubian origin. In Cairo, they chose to live in Heliopolis because prices were relatively low. Her memories of her youth in Heliopolis are of gardens where cicadas sang at night, and of the mosaic of people who were their neighbors: Italians, Jews (who had their seniors' home beside the synagogue), and others. One such neighbor was Alfredo, from Yugoslavia, who arrived at the Heliopolis Sporting Club every day on his horse. Another was the director of the Heliopolis Company's Water Department. He was married to an Italian woman, had a beautiful voice, and planted many of the trees that now adorn the neighborhood.

Hanim had a long and active professional career, working first for Phillips Company and then for the German-language radio in Cairo. Still, she always had time to entertain with her family. And she remembers various cinemas—Normandy, Palace, Oasis, Kashmir (now Heliopolis), and Cinema Roxy, which had two separate theaters. She used to enjoy French coffee at the famous Groppi. As today, she remarks, sandstorms choked Cairo, but the dust then was yellow, not black with pollution.

Opposite:
Mr. Berge Touloumbadjian

Berge Toulumbadjian was born in Heliopolis. His father was an Armenian refugee who fled from Turkey with his family when he was five. His grandfather was a jeweler, and the profession carried on from father to son until today. His parents lived in different places in Cairo, but returned to Heliopolis when Berge was nineteen. He worked as an apprentice in the Khan al-Khalili area but had long wanted to establish a shop in Heliopolis where he lived, because he believed that the Heliopolitan clientele were appropriate customers for a jeweler. He was right, and the shop he established in 1952 grew into a success. During the time of Gamal Abd al-Nasser, many Armenians left Egypt, and Berge himself contemplated emigrating to Canada with his family. He decided against this, however, because he dreaded leaving behind the people he was so attached to. Open-air cinemas figure prominently in memories of the Heliopolis of his youth. These were the places to go with friends and to see new faces. His son Garen, who runs the neatly appointed jewelry shop next to the Groppi on Sharia al-Ahram (as the Avenue des Pyramides is referred to now), finds the neighborhood a good environment in which to do business; he appreciates the sense of security the closely-knit network of neighboring businesses provides.

Below: Guests arriving at the
Heliopolis Palace Hotel in the
1930s.

Opposite: Boulevard Isma'il, now
Baghdad Street, from
Mr. Emad Baki's collection.

Emad Baki's family have lived in Heliopolis for three generations. His
grandfather was a photography buff: he took pictures of the neighborhood,
put them up for sale, and swapped prints with fellow photographers. Baki,
now in his forties, owns a souvenir shop on the chic Baghdad Street
(previously Boulevard Isma'il), where he sells copies of his grandfather's
photographs, handsomely mounted and framed. It has become quite
fashionable for upscale shops, cafés, and restaurants to give their interiors
a nostalgic feel with these photographs of bygone Heliopolis. Many of the
illustrations in this book come from his collection.

Hagg Abbas, a carpenter, owns a workshop north of the Basilica.
Wearing his crocheted scull-cap, he often sits enjoying a cup of tea in front
of his shop, which lies in a courtyard surrounded by typical 'garden city'
houses whose galleries lead to the apartments above. The courtyard is
busy with craftsmen cutting wood, fitting furniture parts, sanding, polishing
and applying varnish. Hagg Abbas has worked here since 1940. The
courtyard then was nearly the same as today, only less crowded. One
qirsh (piaster) often had the buying power of one pound today. The
monthly rent for a decent apartment was two pounds; today it wouldn't
get you very far. Jews, Armenians, and even a Belgian family lived there.
All left, one by one. New people came from all around Egypt, but his own
life, reflects Hagg Abbas, has not changed much.

Above: Hagg Abbas

Opposite: Ever since Heliopolis's early days, the "Garden City" buildings on Damanhur Street have continued to be a busy place for crafts and trade as well as home to the craftspeople and traders.

The owner of one of the numerous jewelry shops near Heliopolis's oldest mosque knows little about the old days here. Like others in the neighborhood, he is a newcomer; they all came in the 1980s or 1990s. To learn about the old Heliopolis, he says, you need to go to the Kurba area, close to the Basilica. But a customer who happened to be in the shop is happy to talk about the neighborhood in the old days, even though she is too young to remember it herself. Her uncle is married to a Frenchwoman, who has become a true Heliopolitan now after having spent most of her long life in the area. Her own mother was born here— to the family of a lawyer on Alexandria Street—and remembers the olden days as a time of splendor, with women in fancy dresses on Sunday outings. Streets were not as crowded as they are today and the community was international.

Opposite: Heliopolis's first mosque located on Mosque Square.

Above: Shops on Harun al-Rashid Street (formerly Rue San Stefano) sell everything from gold jewelry to household utensils.

ELEGANT SPACES

Heliopolis had 2,500 permanent inhabitants in 1912. They were served by one butcher, one *pastier*, a dairy shop, a grocer, one pharmacy, a cigarette shop, a hairdresser, one European and two Arab bakeries, two garment sellers, and two bazaars. There were also four bars, two restaurants, and a grillroom. This, of course, was impressive for an area that five years earlier had been nothing but desert, but still, judging from this description, one might imagine that this small community lived the life of a village. Yet, from the beginning, Heliopolis was a real city. It grew rapidly as more inhabitants moved in and by 1930, it already had about fifty doctors, seven dentists, thirteen chemists, as well as about twenty architects and contractors.

What made Baron Empain's creation a city was not its size, however, but its people. They formed a rich mosaic of different nationalities and cultural backgrounds, religions, and social strata. The focal points for the different communities were places of worship, schools, and religious missions. By 1923, Heliopolis already had twenty-three primary schools, two of which were Catholic (one fee-paying, the other not), two Greek Orthodox, and three Muslim (two of them government-owned) schools for boys. For girls, the choice included a government school, Sacré Coeur School, the Italian School, Notre Dame de Délivrance School, Notre Dame of the Apostles School, and a boarding school. The schools were usually located on or near the premises of a religious establishment.

Opposite: Sacre Coeur School on its eponymous Sacre Coeur Street.

Above: The view of the Heliopolis Palace Hotel from the corner balcony on Boulevard Abbas (now Baghdad Street) hasn't changed much since the 1920s.

Some of Heliopolis's places of worship.

Below: Greek Orthodox church of the Virgin, '

Opposite: Coptic Orthodox church of St. Mark , Rustum al-Alfi mosque, Maronite church of St. Rita, Coptic Catholic church of the Sacred Heart, Greek Catholic (Melkite) church of Immaculate Conception, Prince Hussain Mosque.

Heliopolis offered a compelling choice of places to worship. In addition to the Basilica, there were four other Roman Catholic churches in 1930, a Greek Catholic church just around the corner from a synagogue, Coptic Orthodox, Armenian, and Greek Orthodox churches, a Maronite church and mission, an Anglican Church, the American and the African missions, as well as three mosques. The oldest mosque was located in the heart of the "indigenous" zone on Midan al-Gami' (Mosque Square), which carries the same name today. Although Heliopolis is less cosmopolitan than it used to be, it remains home to quite a few different religious communities. The variety of early Heliopolis society is reflected in the Heliopolis Company's registers. Property owners were a mixture of French, British, Germans, and Italians, in addition to Armenians, Jews, Greeks, and both Christian and Muslim Egyptians. Interestingly, there was apparently no direct correlation between the nationality and religion of people who lived in a particular neighborhood and the people who owned the property there.

The original Heliopolis was designed for people with a European outlook and with European lifestyles. The garden-loving British could appreciate the villas near the Sporting Club; the French could feel at home in the urban and urbane landscape of the boulevards, within walking distance of the gourmet restaurants of the Heliopolis Palace Hotel. Other foreigners were mostly Belgian, German, and Italian, and sometimes American, too. These people belonged to the middle class of bourgeois society and often held senior or middle positions in the quasi-colonial administration. Many well-to-do engineers, lawyers, and other professionals also resided here. The Europeans set the tone in Heliopolis, but it would be completely wrong to see it as a settlement of colonials external to local society. In 1914, one fifth of the 16,000 inhabitants were foreigners; this was the key to Baron Empain's success. Heliopolis perfectly suited Egypt's bourgeoisie and its professionals, both Muslim and Christian, who were part of a rapidly modernizing society. They were also encouraged by the example of the aristocracy, including several members of the royal family, who chose to take up residency here.

Similarly, the lower-income "indigenous" area of 'garden city' apartments and working-class bungalows north of the Basilica were not segregated religiously, ethnically, or socially. While most residents were Egyptian and Muslim, interspersed among them were a significant number of Syrians and Lebanese from the Levant, people from the Balkans, Greeks, and Italians. In addition, among the craftsmen and artisans—the builders, carpenters, plumbers, and cabinetmakers indispensable to any urban area, and especially a growing and expanding one—were people from other European countries. These were the neighbors of the Jews, Armenians, and Copts who tended to live in the wealthier northeastern part of Heliopolis. One discrete block in the "indigenous city" was occupied for a long time by Nubians. The lower-income neighborhoods were peripheral only for a short time: after the First World War they were soon surrounded and swallowed up as Heliopolis expanded north.

Opposite: View from Osman Ibn Affan Stret (formerly Rue de Tanta) on the Basilica.

Above: The garden of the Heliopolis Palace Hotel, 1920s.

To this day, the part of the original Heliopolis once tactfully designated "indigenous," but now called "upper Heliopolis" by some long established expatriates, still hosts many of the district's artisans and servicemen. Alongside carpenters like Hagg Abbas, glass-workers, picture-framers, plumbers, locksmiths, wall-painters, hardware stores, car mechanics, and spare parts dealers have all set up shop. From here people come to the rescue after domestic disasters such as broken water pumps or malfunctioning gas stoves.

The food market the Heliopolis Company built in the early days is also still there. Just as in 1912, chicken, ducks, geese, and pigeons sit in crates made from the ribs of palm fronds, waiting to be sold, slaughtered, and plucked. Carcasses of red meat hang on butchers' hooks, covered with spotless white cloth to protect against flies, while grills sell kebab conveniently nearby so that clients can see that the meat is fresh. Fishmongers assure customers their product comes straight from Alexandria, then after a sale, clean and pack it neatly. If the client wishes, the fish can be grilled on the spot in a spicy seasoning. The smell of fish grilling in the street mixes with the scent of the apple-flavored tobacco that crinkles in waterpipes and with the aroma of coffee—roasted, ground, and packed in old-fashioned paper bags in roasteries nearby.

Heliopolis is not economically segregated, however. Similarly picturesque vegetable markets and workshops can also be found a few steps from the expensive shops in the district's core, while jewelers have taken over shops across from the old market among the fish and poultry. There, village women sell vine leaves, garlic, limes, and okra on the sidewalk in front of shops dealing in diamonds.

Still, the chic shops have always nestled beneath the colonnaded arcades of Heliopolis's main streets: Boulevard Abbas, Boulevard Ismail (today Ibrahim al-Laqqani and Baghdad Streets) and Boulevard Ibrahim (whose name for some mysterious reason remains unchanged). A few of the old establishments were able to survive even the difficult years of the sixties and seventies, and continue to operate until today. For generations of children, the Christo toy shop on Baghdad Street has been a trove resplendent with any treasure desired and, later, once the children are grown up, a place to buy toys for their own children. Another example is the Anglo-Egyptian Shop grocery, whose interior is stacked with shelves up to the very high ceiling. The same very short shop attendant for twenty-five years has performed incredible acrobatic feats to reach the top shelves, skillfully maneuvering his tall ladder while the proprietress reigns at the counter.

Opposite: Fruit and vegetables
vendors in Harun al-Rashid Street;

Above: The arcades of Baghdad
Street house the Anglo-Egyptian
Shop grocery, the Christo toy
shop, Everyman's bookstore, and
other landmark establishments.

Another former Heliopolitan landmark was Home-made Cakes on Baghdad Street, whose customers still fondly remember its tasty croissants and cakes. In 1976, its Swiss owner sold it to Swiss Air, who renamed it Chantilly. Its customers continued to buy the shop's bread and cakes, along with honey sold in pretty jars wrapped Swiss-style in red-and-white checkered cloth. The honey, they believed, was Swiss, although it in fact came from Fayyum. The new owners installed first a few tables to serve sweets, then a bar, then soon the tables became a restaurant and the bar a meeting point for the local community. The Egyptian owners who took over in 1996 have continued the tradition.

Edward, who has run the bar for more than twenty years, recalls that in the early 1980s his clients were mostly Americans working for various contractors. By the mid-1980s, these had been largely replaced by British customers working on the giant Cairo Wastewater Project. Squabbles between English and Irish customers were not infrequent. The British continue to come to the Chantilly bar to this day, although they now work mainly for oil companies and as teachers for the numerous English-language schools. Many other nationals also come, though most patrons are Egyptian. Since the 1990s business has slowed down as the younger crowd, who see Chantilly as old-fashioned, frequent more fashionable places that have since been established in the area.

Above: Ibrahim al-Laqqani Street
(formerly Boulevard Abbas)
choked with traffic.

Opposite: Trendy new outlets seek
traditionally prestigious locations
like al-Kurba.

Not far from Chantilly, on the corner of al-Ahram and Ibrahim al-Laqqani Streets, sits L'Amphytryon, a restaurant whose pleasant outdoors section was dubbed the Biergarten a few years ago by a group of German conservators who lived nearby.

Establishments like these, however, have been slowly dying out as anachronisms in twenty-first century Heliopolis. A cellular telephone outlet recently replaced the landmark Armenian pharmacy at the corner of Baghdad and Ibrahim streets, where for many years an unbelievably large Persian cat lay sleeping almost continuously in the display window.

As more and more long-established businesses closed up shop, as historic buildings were torn down and replaced with nondescript structures, and as once-elegant boulevards filled with crowds of peddlers selling trinkets and other cheap wares, it sometimes seemed that Baron Empain's Paris-in-a-desert-oasis had slipped into ever-accelerating decline. Yet, in recent years, there have been indications that this may not be true. The Heliopolis Association has played an important role in tidying up the streets. The centennial celebrations in 2005 went ahead in the festive spirit reminiscent of the city's early years. In many instances on the main commercial streets, new upscale shops and fashionable cafés have begun replacing the older establishments, attracting the young and trendy as their clientele. This crowd is very different from what the Baron could ever have imagined. Many of the shops are outlets for world chains and can be found just as easily in other Cairo districts. And the streets are just as crowded. Yet still, the unique architecture keeps the special, inimitable spirit of the place alive. The Baron's dream has been realized: the empty desert plateau has been transformed into an oasis.

A DAY ENDS

Heliopolis goes to bed late. In summer, streets stay busy late at night, and many shops don't close until one or two in the morning. Slowly, though, the streets empty of people, and finally even the cats—nocturnal creatures by nature—disappear. At that point, the back streets and gardens are taken over by weasels—which in the daytime are only rarely seen darting for shelter under parked cars. In the sky, huge owls glide soundlessly between trees and buildings, their pale grey plumage glowing stark white in the darkness. All kinds of chirping, buzzing and chattering animals crawl out of their holes and even an occasional scorpion scampers across the tiny gardens, in front of which thousands of people shop each day. Huge, crow-sized fruit bats feast on mangoes in trees where a mere century ago lay nothing but barren, lifeless desert. Looking at Heliopolis in the small hours of the morning helps one to see how, in a very real sense, Baron Empain created a true oasis, where now so many different creatures live together.

Photographs: Patrick Godeau, pages 3, 6, 51, 72, 91, 98, 99, 100, 102, 103, 104, 105, 108, 109, 110, 111, 114, 115, 117, 121, 127, 134, 135, 137, 142, 144, 145, 147, 148, 149, 150, 151, 154, 160, 165, 167, 171, 173, 174, 176, 177 (churches), 178, 180, 181, 184, 185, 188; Agnieszka Dobrowolska and Jarosław Dobrowolski, pages 4, 19, 32, 47, 49, 68, 74, 76, 78, 80, 81, 86, 90, 106, 107, 112, 113, 118, 119, 120, 123, 125, 136, 139, 141, 146, 152, 155, 156, 158, 170, 172, 177 (mosques), 182, 183, 186; Michael Jones, pages 19, 22; Matjaž Kačičnik, pages 53, 55, 57, 59, 61, 63, 65, 67.

Sources of reproduced material: courtesy of the Environmental and Remote Sensing Services Center, Heliopolis, pages 8–9; Georg Ebers, *Egypt: Descriptive, Historical and Picturesque*, 1879 (courtesy of the American Research Center in Egypt Library), pages 10, 30; Claude-Louis Fourmont, *Carte Topographique vue en perspective des plaines d'Heliopolis et de Memphis*, 1754 (courtesy of the German Archaeological Institute in Cairo Library) pages 12–13; drawings by Pascal Coste (courtesy of the Bibliothèque Municipale de Marseille) pages 14, 16, 28, 138; *Description de l'Egypte ou recueil des observations et des recherches*, 1822 (courtesy of the American Research Center in Egypt Library) pages 7, 15, 25, 27, 190, 191; Sebastian Münster, *Cosmographia*, 1574, pages 20, 22–23; courtesy of the Heliopolis Company Archive, pages 34–35, 43, 44, 46, 70–71, 92–93, 96–97, 101, 122–23, 124–25, 126–27, 128–29, 130, 131, 132, 133, 163, 168, 169, 175, 179; courtesy of Samir Rafaat, pages 38, 143; courtesy of Virgin Graphics archives, pages 39, 78, 79, 83, 84, 85; authors' collection, pages 52, 54, 56, 58, 60, 62, 64, 66, 94, 162; *l'Architecture*, vol.16: 1903, No 15, pages 88, 89.

Line drawings: Jarosław Dobrowolski

Title calligraphy: Jarosław Dobrowolski